GROUP THERAPY FOR VOICE HEARERS

Based on extensive interviews with expert facilitators from around the world and grounded in empirical evidence, *Group Therapy for Voice Hearers* includes numerous tips, strategies, case examples, and reflection questions to bring the material to life in a practical way.

Chapters address the need for practical, accessible training in how to facilitate sessions and identify six key factors that lead to a successful session: safety, flexibility, empowerment, the integration of lived experience, self-awareness, and attention to the needs of the group process.

This book is an important resource for mental health professionals working with clients who hear voices.

Andrea D. Lefebvre, PsyD, LPC-ALPS, is a Licensed Clinical Psychologist at Northwood Health Systems in Wheeling, West Virginia, and has lived experience as a former voice hearer. She is also a treatment team member of Quiet Minds, a first episode psychosis program in Northern West Virginia.

Richard W. Sears, PsyD, PhD, MBA, ABPP, is a Board-Certified Clinical Psychologist in private practice in Cincinnati, Ohio. He is an international speaker and author on mindfulness and psychotherapy.

Jennifer M. Ossege, PsyD, is a Licensed Clinical Psychologist and co-founder of Viewpoint Psychological Services, PLLC, a group practice offering counseling and psychological services. She also teaches at Xavier University and Union Institute & University in Cincinnati, Ohio.

GROUP THERAPY FOR VOICE HEARERS

Insights and Perspectives

Andrea D. Lefebvre,
Richard W. Sears, and
Jennifer M. Ossege

Routledge
Taylor & Francis Group
NEW YORK AND LONDON

First published 2019
by Routledge
52 Vanderbilt Avenue, New York, NY 10017

and by Routledge
2 Park Square, Milton Park, Abingdon, Oxon, OX14 4RN

Routledge is an imprint of the Taylor & Francis Group, an informa business

Library of Congress Cataloging-in-Publication Data
A catalog record for this title has been requested

ISBN: 978-1-138-50063-1 (hbk)
ISBN: 978-1-138-50064-8 (pbk)
ISBN: 978-1-315-14591-4 (ebk)

Typeset in Baskerville
by Deanta Global Publishing Services, Chennai, India

To the members of my Voices and Visions group, both past and present:
Your bravery and humor inspire me.

CONTENTS

ABOUT THE AUTHORS

Andrea D. Lefebvre, PsyD, LPC-ALPS, is a Clinical Psychologist who specializes in trauma, substance abuse, and psychosis-related disorders at a community mental health center in Wheeling, West Virginia, and is a clinical supervisor at a crisis stabilization unit in Weirton, West Virginia, which specializes in both substance abuse and mental health issues. She has experience facilitating groups for voice hearers in outpatient psychiatric settings. Additionally, Dr. Lefebvre has lived experience with voice hearing and is a therapist with Quiet Minds, an organization that provides clinical and consultation services for young people with first episode psychosis. Dr. Lefebvre has clinical experience working in community mental health agencies, inpatient psychiatric units, residential treatment facilities, and school-based therapy programs.

Dr. Lefebvre earned her Master's degree in Art Therapy and Counseling at Ursuline College, Ohio, and her Doctorate in Clinical Psychology from Union Institute & University, Ohio. She is a Licensed Clinical Counselor in both Ohio and West Virginia, and an Approved Licensed Professional Supervisor in Counseling in West Virginia. She authored the doctoral dissertation: *What Makes Auditory Verbal Hallucinations Groups Effective? A Qualitative Analysis of Insights from Group Facilitators Regarding the Mechanisms of Change.*

Richard W. Sears, PsyD, PhD, MBA, ABPP, is a Board-Certified Clinical Psychologist in Cincinnati, Ohio, where he runs a private psychology and consultation practice. He regularly gives workshops across the US on topics related to psychotherapy and mindfulness. He is an annual adjunct professor at the University of Cincinnati, a volunteer Professor of Psychiatry and Behavioral Neurosciences at the UC College of Medicine, Ohio, and a Research/Psychologist Contractor with the Cincinnati VA Medical Center.

Dr. Sears is the author of *The Sense of Self: Perspectives from Science and Zen Buddhism*; *Mindfulness: Living Through Challenges and Enriching Your Life in this Moment*; *Building Competence in Mindfulness-Based Cognitive Therapy*; *Mindfulness in Clinical Practice*; *Mindfulness-Based Cognitive Therapy for Posttraumatic Stress Disorder*; and *Consultation Skills for Mental Health Professionals*. He is a co-editor of the books *Perspectives on Spirituality and Religion in Psychotherapy* and *The Resilient Mental Health Practice: Nourishing Your Business, Your Clients, and Yourself*. His website is www.psych-insights.com.

Jennifer M. Ossege, PsyD, is a Licensed Clinical Psychologist in the Commonwealth of Kentucky and specializes in the treatment of trauma. She is the co-founder and managing partner of Viewpoint Psychological Services, PLLC, a group private practice with three office locations in the Northern Kentucky/Greater Cincinnati area. Dr. Ossege oversees both administrative operations and clinical practice, supervises early career clinicians, and maintains an active client caseload, serving a wide range of clients in the Greater Cincinnati area. She has been a regular adjunct faculty member in the Psychology Department at Xavier University in Cincinnati, Ohio, since 2003, working with both undergraduate and graduate students. Dr. Ossege earned her Master's degree in Clinical Psychology as well as her Doctoral degree (PsyD) in Clinical Psychology from Xavier University. She has been on the faculty of Union Institute & University since 2010, where she has taught in the Doctor of Psychology (PsyD) Program, the Masters of Organizational Leadership Program (MSOL), and the Bachelor's Degree Program. In her faculty role at Union Institute & University, Dr. Ossege served on the dissertation committee for Dr. Lefebvre's research project: *What Makes Auditory Verbal Hallucinations Groups Effective? A Qualitative Analysis of Insights from Group Facilitators Regarding the Mechanisms of Change.*

Dr. Ossege is the lead editor of *The Resilient Mental Health Practice: Nourishing Your Business, Your Clients, and Yourself,* and she is a co-author of *Perspectives and Hopes of Muslim American Women: The Paradox of Honor.* Her practice website is www.viewpointpsych.com.

ACKNOWLEDGMENTS

This book is dedicated to Dr. Brooke Wolf, who helped during a difficult time; Dr. Perry Stanley, who taught me the value of a "non-anxious presence" and the value of systems; Dr. Ron Rielly (just because I'm using your full title doesn't mean I like you any less), who always encourages me to be myself and never to take research at face value; my parents, Fred and Ruth, who taught me about love and patience; AND FINALLY: this book is for the playful, kind, and wise group members (past and present) of my weekly Voices group! You inspire me.

INTRODUCTION

As I sit down to write this introduction, I am amazed by how my life has come full circle within the past six years. In July 2012, while in my doctorate program for psychology, I went through a tough time personally: a sexual assault, a disappointing breakup with a guy I liked, working full time, and attending full-time classes as a doctoral student took their toll on me. Shortly after the sexual assault, I developed acute psychotic disorder. I began hearing voices, some friendly and supportive, and others which told me I was unsafe. I took off in my car, thinking I was being chased by Middle Eastern terrorists, threw my cell phone into an abandoned lot (so the supposed terrorists couldn't follow me), and was convinced my parents were unsafe to be around. Thankfully, I did not have my headlights on that night, which somehow led to a cop pulling me over. I ended up telling him my fears about terrorists chasing me, and he took me to a local hospital. I spent the night in the hospital, my parents showing up the next morning, and voluntarily admitted myself to an inpatient psychiatric ward later that day. During my stay in the psychiatric hospital, I remember sitting on the floor by my bed, and my voices (or, during this particular instance, one voice, who I called "grandma") saying, "This is a test. You are being tested. Richard Sears and Jennifer Ossege will help you. They will rescue you."

So, a little backstory: *Dr. Richard Sears* and *Dr. Jennifer Ossege* were two professors in my doctorate program, but I did not know them well. I kind of knew Dr. Ossege from a personality assessment course I recently started, and I did not know much about Dr. Sears. However, my voices convinced me that these two professors were going to help me, and in my addled brain I believed they would *literally* remove me from the psychiatric facility. (As my head cleared, I realized this was obviously not going to happen.) I have never told them this story (until now), and years later I was lucky enough to have them on my dissertation committee. Maybe the voices represented my intuition or subconscious guiding me to the people who would best help me. Maybe the voices were something more mystical—who knows. Richard and Jennifer later encouraged me to turn my dissertation into this book, which I never would have anticipated. I did not tell them the personal connection to my dissertation until I was nearly ready to defend. I am now lucky enough to have Richard and Jennifer as my co-authors. Apparently, my voices were prescient and knew something I didn't at the time: Jennifer and Richard rescued me in their own way by encouraging me to write this book, and in the process, to no longer feel ashamed of this part of my life. Telling my story no longer holds an emotional charge. It's just a series of memories which I can call upon to help others. Speaking of ...

Back to my psychiatric hospitalization—what struck me was how little therapy I received while hospitalized. I gave them blood—lots of it—and was placed on lithium, which left me drooling, dazed, and restless. A well-meaning therapist type (I'm still unsure what her role was) met with me during the first day I was admitted to the psychiatric ward, asked me about what led me to being admitted, and I did not see or speak with her again until the day of my discharge. There were a couple of therapy groups—I vaguely remember an art therapy group and another group on nutrition (or maybe feelings?)—I'm unsure. I was a licensed therapist prior to my meltdown, so I was familiar with group therapy. Hell, I ran therapy groups in multiple settings, including hospitals and residential treatment centers prior to my hospitalization.

During this time, I spoke more with clients than staff. A few mental health technicians would occasionally chat with me, and the psychiatrist met briefly with me every few days. I felt like I was in a holding pen as staff waited for the "meds to kick in." Techs would observe me and fellow clients from behind a glassed-in office. It would have been nice if they had come out and mingled with us clients. When I was a mental health tech (yep—held that job too during my master's training), we were expected to mingle with clients "on the floor." Therefore, this type of treatment made me feel like "my crazy" was possibly contagious, or that the techs thought we clients would lose control, attack them, and defecate on the dining room table. (There were a few fellow clients on the ward who seemed like likely candidates. One young guy, another client, took a shine to me and followed me around the unit. Sort of flattering, as he looked like Jennifer Lopez's then boyfriend. However, he lost points in my mind when I saw him screaming into the phone, and he later exposed himself to a nurse. No bueno, cute fellow psych patient—no psych ward romance for us. (Don't worry—I'd never hook up with a fellow client. Although—FYI: psych wards are hotbeds for hookups.)

Eventually, I was deemed healthy enough to be released to my parents' custody. My job required I have a psychologist evaluate me before returning to work. I passed with flying colors, but the whole experience left me very disillusioned and confused about how voice hearers were treated in psychiatric hospitals. My outpatient psychiatrist, a very calm and understanding woman, listened to my concerns about the side effects the medications gave me: drooling, brain fog, insomnia, agitation, decreased processing speed, and poor concentration skills. Thankfully, she adjusted my meds until I was feeling like my normal "non-voice hearing" self once more.

I was determined to return to classes, and although cautious about my plans, my psychiatrist was supportive. Back on track at school and work, I headed into my second year of doctoral studies. Reluctantly, I decreased my work hours to part time and began working as a practicum student at a community mental health clinic. While at this clinic, I began co-facilitating an intensive outpatient therapy group (IOP) and found myself personally benefiting from the rhythm and containment provided by this environment. I began to notice that clients who reported psychosis-related symptoms during their assessments or to their therapists did not mention these symptoms in the IOP groups. My curiosity about clients' reticence to share their psychosis-related symptoms was the seed of this book. In an unusual bit of synchronicity (one of many over the upcoming years), I was invited to develop a "hearing voices" group with other clinicians. This experience informed my decision to conduct my dissertation research on facilitators' opinions about what makes hearing voices groups effective.

In another cool bit of synchronicity, around the time I was looking into developing a group for voice hearers, my Biological Bases of Behavior professor, Dr. Lewis Mehl-Madrona, introduced my cohort to the Hearing Voices Network and the International Society for Psychological and Social Approaches to Psychosis (ISPS). Both resources were a treasure trove of information, and looking at these organization's websites felt empowering. They promoted treating voice hearers in a non-pathologizing and thoughtful manner. I would later attend the ISPS International Conference in New York City, which was so empowering! Voice hearers and researchers from all over the world converged to discuss their ideas about working with voice hearers in a respectful, progressive way—informed by research! People were doing such wonderful research about working with voice hearers, and were not simply focusing on eliminating these psychological experiences in people.

As I finished up my doctoral studies, I began to heal emotionally. I worked regularly with my trusted psychiatrist. I was accepted into a pre-doctoral internship in West Virginia, where another synchronistic moment occurred. I learned that one of my clinical supervisors had been asked to be the clinical director (along with his wife, who is a therapist) for West Virginia's inaugural first episode psychosis program, Quiet Minds. My clinical supervisor was well-versed in psychosis! What?!

Over the next three years, I had a lot of ups and downs regarding my life in Wheeling, West Virginia. Professionally, things were great: I graduated with my PsyD, was hired by the agency where I interned, and was licensed in West Virginia as a psychologist. But holy crap, did I go through it personally! I weathered scary health care issues (e.g., two cancer scares, several related invasive procedures, and subsequent surgery), the death of two beloved cats within a six-month span, friend betrayals, multiple family legal issues, a ton of unexpected medical and tax bills, family health scares/issues, and every clinician's nightmare—the unexpected suicide of a client. My friends and family were available largely long-distance, but sometimes when bad news showed up, I just needed a hug. Unfortunately, because I was far away from my support people, hugs had to be delayed.

In spite of all the things I went through, my emotional reactivity began to decrease and my connection with my higher power grew. Left to my own devices and limited financial resources (thanks, medical bills!), I had a lot of time to think. And read. And meditate. And nap (lots of napping). Limited distractions. I meditated, developed an obsession with pepperoni rolls (a West Virginian delicacy), and fell in love with the rivers and mountains of the Ohio Valley. I regularly spoke with my supervisors at work, whose compassionate presence helped to ground me.

Also, the more I shared my story about hearing voices, the stronger I felt, which also contributed to my overall decreased anxiety. I began telling my supervisors and then colleagues about my past voice hearing experiences and how these experiences shaped me as a clinician. I was lucky to have a group of thoughtful mental health professionals and mentors who showed interest in my story and offered a non-anxious presence as I shared my story.

Nowadays, I am a licensed psychologist and supervisor, and a clinical director of a crisis unit for folks who are struggling with their own mental health crises. I work with the Quiet Minds first episode psychosis program, see clients, run groups (one for voice hearers, naturally), and eat way too much food (people love to bake WAY too much here). My social circle has expanded, and I feel less isolated.

I moved from skepticism about the "power of sharing one's story" to firmly believing. This therapy s__ works! I'm living proof! Hopefully this book will guide interested facilitators in how to work with people who hear voices, and to do so in a compassionate way. This book is not a step-by-step guide for how to work with voice hearers. Use whatever theoretical orientation is clinically relevant: Cognitive Behavioral Therapy for Psychosis (CBTp), Acceptance and Commitment Therapy for Psychosis (ACTp), Psychodynamic Theory, etc. What I hope this book can address is *the attitude and style* with which we wield these therapeutic tools as group facilitators. I spoke with ten different facilitators from all over the world to discuss how they run hearing voices type groups. In this book, I share the themes from these interviews, my experiences as a facilitator, and my own lived experiences. I have intentionally used person-centered language, so I use the terms "voices and visions" or "voices" instead of hallucinations. Over the years, I have been taught the power of non-pathologizing language. Some of the facilitators I interviewed use the expression "extreme state experiences" instead of "psychosis," as they reason an "extreme" experience led to such a state. My use of client-centered language is not to sound pompous or sanctimonious. It's only to highlight a simple truth which my colleague, Dr. Perry Stanley, often says: "We have more in common with these people we call clients than we do differences."

I couldn't agree more, Dr. Stanley, I couldn't agree more!

1

CONSIDERATIONS FOR NON-VOICE HEARERS

Understanding the Continuum of Human Experiences

> *Reflection: What shifts in thinking are necessary to facilitate a group with people who experience different phenomena than you have experienced? How can you ensure that your own biases and perceptions do not negatively impact the group process?*

Throughout this book, Dr. Andrea Lefebvre will share her unique perspectives of what it is like from the inside to hear voices and see visions. She has been able to turn her personal challenges into expertise in helping others. In this chapter, I will share some insights that have helped me (RWS) as a non-voice hearer in working with this population.

To begin with, be sure you are ready for this journey. I recently saw a posting in a listserv asking, "I have a client with voices and visions, and I have never worked with that before. Any tips?" My tip was, basically, "Don't work with that person!" These are human lives, not practice targets. While this book will provide inspiration and direction, be sure to get the training, supervision, and/or consultation you need before working with clients.

If you happen to be a non-voice hearer, it can be challenging to understand what it is like to experience voices, visions, and paranoia. The guiding principle to keep in mind is that as human beings, we have far more commonalities than we have differences. As you begin to delve into extreme state experiences with people, it can bring up some very deep philosophical and existential questions, in both you and the individuals with whom you work. These questions can be very deep and profound, and have been considered by humans since they have been able to think in words:

- What is the nature of perception?
- What is the nature of thought?
- If I cannot trust my own thoughts and feelings, what can I trust?
- What is reality?
- Am I the only one who thinks and perceives this way?
- Who am I?
- Am I a certain single strand of experience, or multiple "selves," or the totality of what is going on?
- Is there a deeper spiritual connection that we all share that most people do not notice?

If these questions are in your mind, you may not be very concerned about the rather mundane things being discussed in the conversations around you. Similarly, if you have ever had a close call with death, you recognize that much of what previously seemed important is no longer a big deal to you.

Imagine having an extreme state experience in which your thinking and perceptions are significantly altered from what you have previously experienced, and very different from other people around you. The human mind seeks to understand and make sense of these questions and experiences. It is hard to argue with what your senses tell you, so you desperately try to figure out what is going on. When the experience seems extreme, then extreme explanations make sense, even though they would not occur to you at other times. When science and logic cannot provide answers, you might seek to explore magical and spiritual explanations. If you heard voices in your head, it would seem a logical possibility that aliens with superior technology were trying to communicate with you. Perhaps you have become able to perceive the voices of those who have passed away, or even of angels or demons. If you could see things that others could not see, it would make sense that perhaps you had developed the ability to perceive other dimensions of existence.

You might even feel that your perceptions are a gift of heightened sensitivity. And who is the authority to say whether or not this is true? As a fifth-degree black belt martial artist, I can tell when someone is about to punch me long before they do it, because I have practiced and observed others for many years. Through my heightened sensitivity, I can pick up on things about a person's body that they themselves do not even notice.

Recently, I went with my daughter to a Lego® store. She found a bin full of "surprise grab bag" Harry Potter figures. She desperately was hoping for one of two specific figures, and she asked me to try to somehow sense which one contained Dumbledore or Voldemort. Since there were 22 possible figures, we had a 1 in 11 chance of getting one of them. A store employee noticed our dilemma, and said he was lucky at picking out characters. He began picking up the small bags and gently squeezing their content. Simply by feeling with his fingertips, he was able to tell us who was in each bag, and he gave us both of the characters my daughter wanted. When we opened the bags after buying them, the employee had been 100% correct! It was like magic!

Much of our current technology would have looked like magic to someone living a hundred years ago. It would make sense that "magic" is indeed a logical consideration if you could clearly perceive a different reality with your senses. And yet, you live in a society that does not value such experiences or explanations. In fact, people may think you are broken, and may even be afraid of you. Society no longer burns people at the stake, but it may shun you into complete isolation, and may even take away your civil liberties.

You would long to be understood. You would long to be heard. You would long to find other like-minded individuals with whom you could share your experiences. As a human being, you would still have all the emotional needs of a human being, and experience stress just like everyone else. According to the diathesis-stress model, given enough stress, all of us are prone to experiencing mental health challenges. For some, it will lead to anxiety. For others, depression. For some, addiction. For yet others, they will experience voices and visions.

If you are courageous enough to explore the extremes of human perception, you can make a profound difference in the lives of many individuals. And if you are willing to be open to examining your own assumptions, you may even attain some profound breakthroughs in your own life.

If you feel called to facilitate groups for those who have voices and visions, it will be important to realize that human experiences fall on a continuum. Be careful not to dichotomize people into an "us" versus a "them." Aside from medical, genetic, and neurological explanations for extreme state experiences, it will be important to understand that all of us have subjectively experienced similar things, albeit to different degrees.

The Continuum of Sensory Perceptions

When I am teaching Zen, I often ask the question, "What is the truth?" Most people struggle with this question, because they try to answer it intellectually and get lost in thoughts and concepts. When they "come to their senses," the truth appears clearly before them.

Empiricism is what science is about. The word empirical literally means "evident to the senses"—I can touch it, hear it, see it, smell it, or taste it. While thinking can be a helpful tool to devise theories and to make predictions, science aims at an empirical understanding of reality.

However, perception is a complicated and sometimes unreliable process. When our senses are working well, we do not notice the processes in between the reality and the perception. But if I have cataracts, I see my eyes, which may appear as "things" floating out in front of me. If I have tinnitus, I will hear my ears, which I might perceive as a buzzing sound outside of me.

My brain also has a big role in processing my perceptions. The sound of the wind becomes a ghostly whisper. A shadow becomes a potentially threatening creature. A tingle under my skin may be perceived as an attack from something small and unseen. We often recognize sensory illusions for what they are, but sometimes our brains fire up emotions that tell us these thoughts and perceptions are quite real.

These experiences are quite common for all of us in the world of dreaming. We get caught up in emotionally gripping stories all throughout the night (whether or not we remember them when we wake up), even though our external senses are not even operating. The voices and visions we are experiencing are entirely in our brains, but we fully believe them to be reality at the time. Very occasionally, we might even become lucid during a dream, where we know we are dreaming while we are dreaming, but most of us do not realize that what we are experiencing is not "real" until we wake up.

While our daily reality often intrudes into our dreaming state, sometimes dreams intrude into reality. I had a friend who played a lot of Tetris in college, a video game in which you arrange geometric pieces to fit together. One day, she was listening to a lecture in a very sleep-deprived state. She began noticing that the words coming out of the professor's mouth formed shapes, and she was trying to arrange them to fit together as they fell toward the floor.

I was once sleeping over at a friend's house and fell into a deep sleep. In the middle of the night, I sat up and saw what looked like a demon coming out of the wall. I put my arm over my friend and raised my other arm to fend off the demon, which slowly faded away. My friend thanked me in a confusing tone, then rolled over and went back to sleep.

For some people, it is common for thoughts, voices, and visions to intrude into and be confused with "reality," and they do not realize it until their brains change the emotional tone of those experiences.

TVs and Radios

Some individuals feel like they are being spoken to by radios and televisions, and they may even base important decisions on what they hear. This too can be understood to be something we could all experience.

As you are reading these words, chances are you know that I have written them to no one in particular. But what if you were reading this on your phone as a text from "Richard Sears"? You would have a feeling connected to these words, an emotional sense that I am talking directly to you.

When you are listening to the radio, you know the sounds coming out of the speaker are not being directed specifically to you. But if I was calling you on a speaker phone, your brain would fire up a feeling of being spoken to directly. Likewise, when you watch television, you know the images are being projected from a faraway place, and you feel yourself to be a passive observer. But if I connect with you via video conference, your brain will give you a distinct feeling that I am specifically talking to you.

For some people, their brains fire up feelings of connection when they hear the radio or watch television. It is not a logical thing; it is a strong and distinct feeling that most people trust implicitly. I once worked with someone who was continuously angry at the staff on the inpatient unit because he had been involuntarily hospitalized. He was especially angry about being given shots of antipsychotic medication. In one particularly poignant moment in group therapy, he realized, "If the medicine kicks in, it won't feel like the television is talking to me, and I will feel lonely." We can all relate to feeling lonely.

Paranoia

When you see extremes of paranoia, you may wonder why the person does not just respond to the logic of your arguments against it. Here again, this can happen to all of us to different degrees.

Imagine you step outside your work office for a few minutes and you notice that there is a fire in the lobby. You run back in to warn your coworkers, shouting, "There's a fire! We have to evacuate the building!"

To your shock and consternation, your coworkers ask you, "Did you take your medication today?"

"What does that have to do with anything?!?" You reply with urgency. "We have to get out of the building before we all burn up!"

Imagine how you would feel if all your coworkers looked at you with pity and said, "There's no fire—just sit down and finish your work." You just saw the fire in the lobby with your own eyes, and your coworkers were inside the office. How would they know? Out of a desire to save them, you would become more insistent that they needed to evacuate.

However, if they continued to insist that there was no fire, something might flip inside of you—perhaps they are in denial because they are the ones who set the fire! You would then realize you had better not say anything to anyone, because there is a conspiracy going on, and you no longer know who you can trust.

In this example, the best thing would be for someone to just step outside with you for a moment and take a look. If there was no fire, you would at least feel calmer, and perhaps wonder if maybe you got confused by the smell of a cigarette or something.

When I was in graduate school, I worked as a security guard in the evenings. A janitor who worked in the building told me he could hear kids playing in the empty part of the building, and that his ex-wife was back there hiding. At first, I dismissed his concerns since they did not seem logical, which only seemed to make him more upset, and he would mumble at me under his breath. As fate would have it, I had just started learning about paranoia in one of my crisis intervention courses, and I realized I was making things worse by acting like I did not believe him. The next time he hinted that people were in the building, I leaped out and told him I'd go check it out. When I returned, I said that I did not see anyone, but that I would monitor the area and regularly check the computer, which recorded when any door was opened or closed. He thanked me. This lasted a few days, and he became more relaxed. Then, one day, after I jumped up to go check out a concern, he said, "Never mind. I think I'm just imagining things."

When I was a practicum student at a veteran's inpatient unit, I was shadowing a psychiatrist, along with several residents. The psychiatrist was one day interviewing a man who claimed that people were trying to poison him. The psychiatrist was patiently asking questions about who the patient thought was doing this. At one point, a resident student got frustrated and impatient, and burst out, "Why would anyone want to poison you? Don't you think that is all in your mind?" Of course, that is what someone who is trying to poison you would say, so the patient immediately got angry and shut down completely.

I was once working with a young adult who began showing signs that his thinking processes were changing. In one session, I could tell that he was distracted, and he kept looking at my shirt. When I asked him what was going on, he was very hesitant to tell me. He finally said, "I know it sounds silly, but I can't get rid of the thought that the pen in your shirt is a microphone."

It would have been easy for me to dismiss his concerns, or simply tell him that it was obviously not a microphone, or try to talk him out of it. But of course, that is exactly what someone would do if they really did have a microphone and did not want you to know it, so saying those things would have only made the situation worse.

I looked down at the pen and said, "Hmmm—it really does look a lot like the top of a microphone. I can see why you would think that." I then handed the pen to him and invited him to open it up and take a look at it. After doing so, he apologized and said he felt silly, but I expressed appreciation that he shared his feelings with me.

Extreme Mood State Experiences

The theory of mood state-dependent learning and memory tell us that the thoughts, memories, and images in our minds are affected by our mood (Ucros, 1989). When we are in a good mood, we can easily bring to mind happy thoughts. When we are anxious, thoughts and memories related to anxiety easily pop up in our minds. When we are depressed, it is easy to remember all the bad stuff that has happened to us and all the bad choices we have made.

Decades ago, Beck identified what is known as the "cognitive triad" of depressive thinking (Beck, Rush, Shaw, & Emery, 1979). Depression hijacks people's thinking processes. They will develop negative views of the self, of the world, and of the future.

Everyone with clinical depression will think the world is a terrible place, the future is horrible, and that they are inherently bad. However, for some individuals, this thinking can go to an extreme. I have worked with people who were so depressed, they had visions of blood dripping from the walls, or saw skeletons wherever they looked. I worked with a couple of individuals who were even convinced that they were the devil. In their minds, they thought that they were such terrible, horrible, awful people that no creature in the universe could be worse than they were. Hence, the only "logical" explanation was that they must literally be the devil incarnate.

At the opposite end of the mood spectrum, we have all had occasions when we were in such a great mood that we may have over-estimated our abilities. During extreme states of mania, people can come to feel and believe that they are superhuman. They feel like they can do anything, perhaps even fly. They feel so great, they wonder if perhaps they have become a divine being.

Decentering and Defusion

We all have conversations with ourselves. Sometimes these conversations become arguments and become really engaging. We sometimes fight with these thoughts as if there really is another person in our heads. Some of the voices seem more real to us than others. People can spend days or even years fighting their own thoughts or trying to stop themselves from thinking negative thoughts.

Despite your best efforts, you cannot control your own thoughts. Sure, you can influence them and suppress them sometimes, but when you are stressed out or anxious, these thoughts seem continuous. The more you argue with them, the more you become ensnared by them. Trying to stop your thoughts is like trying not to think of a pink elephant. The effort to stop your own thoughts may work temporarily, but the effort increases stress, which tends to increase the intensity of the thoughts in the long run.

Just imagine if those thoughts increased in volume and intensity to the point where they took the form of actual voices inside your head, or seemingly outside your head. You would likely feel compelled to argue and/or to try to stop these voices. Imagine trying to ignore a voice that is always wanting to talk to you, often at the worst times. It would be like being in a movie theater next to someone who won't stop talking during the movie, making it hard to be fully present.

All of us have thoughts that we think are literally true. However, the fact is that everything we perceive is a state of the nervous system. When you watch a movie, you tend to forget that it is nothing more than flickering electronic images, and you get pulled into the drama and the emotions. Likewise, we all tend to get caught up in the drama of our own thoughts, even though thoughts are simply words inside our heads that have no physical reality. In a similar way, individuals who hear voices and see visions have trouble recognizing that they are projections of the mind.

Third-wave cognitive-behavioral therapies like Acceptance and Commitment Therapy (Hayes, Strosahl, & Wilson, 2012) and Mindfulness-Based Cognitive Therapy (Segal, Williams, & Teasdale, 2013) teach that rather than arguing with thoughts or trying to stop them, we learn to see them for what they are. They are mental events. The process is known as "decentering" or "defusion." Most people feel like they are in the center of their thoughts or are fused to their thoughts. When they have a thought like, "I am a terrible person," they feel strong emotions, memories, and associations attached to it. However, clients can learn to see thoughts only as words in their heads, not as absolute truth. Clients learn to recognize, "I am having a thought that I am a terrible person—that is not who I am." Instead of getting lost in the movie like it is really happening, they step back and remember that it is just a movie. When you see it for what it is, you can make a more conscious choice about whether or not the thought is helpful or not.

This decentering or defusion process can also be helpful with voices and visions. I once had a young client with schizophrenia who went fishing. At one point, he caught a big fish, and as he was holding it in his hand, it started talking to him. The client was able to step back and tell himself, "Whoa—I'm having a hallucination!" Rather than getting lost in the experience and conversing with the fish, or getting freaked out about it, he took it as a sign that his illness was worsening. He proactively went to his psychiatrist and had his medications adjusted, preventing things from getting worse.

Presence

Finally, one of the most powerful things you can do as a therapist is to be present with your clients. To have a real, human, authentic encounter. When I worked on inpatient units, I often observed that other clinicians were afraid of the patients with whom they were working. These people are human beings, and as bizarre as some of their experiences may seem at times, they crave human contact and presence. If you stay present, you may even find yourself privileged to some new dimensions of human experience, which is a very rare gift.

Summary Points

- Facilitators who are "non-voice hearers" can benefit by considering ways in which all people are similar, rather than focusing solely on differences. Gaining perspective and supervision is important to ensure you do not practice outside your scope of competence.
- Experiences vary wildly, and those who hear voices and have extreme state experiences may feel paranoid or believe that they have special knowledge, etc. Considering things from

the client's perspective (trying to understand the client's reality) is important.

- Processes such as decentering or defusion can be helpful in understanding and dealing with voices and visions.
- Being present, genuinely authentically so, with clients is one of the most effective strategies that facilitators can engage in.

References

Beck, A. T., Rush, A. J., Shaw, B. F., & Emery, G. (1979). *Cognitive therapy for depression.* New York: The Guilford Press, p. 11.

Hayes, S. C., Strosahl, K., & Wilson, K. G. (2012). *Acceptance and commitment therapy: The process and practice of mindful change.* New York: Guilford Press.

Segal, Z., Williams, M., & Teasdale, J. (2013). *Mindfulness-based cognitive therapy for depression* (2nd ed.). New York: Guilford Press.

Ucros, G. (1989). Mood state-dependent memory: A meta-analysis. *Cognition & Emotion, 3*(2), 139–169.

2

VOICE HEARING

Stigma and Treatment

> *Reflection: What do you see as the challenges of recovery for those who hear voices and have extreme state experiences? How can you help as a facilitator working with this population?*

Prevalence and Problems with Medication

Did you know mental health researchers estimate the frequency of people who experience voices (in the general population) is between 5% and 28% (de Leede-Smith & Barkus, 2013; Johns, Cannon, Singleton, Murray, Farrell, Brugha et al., 2004; Scott, Chant, Andrews, & McGrath, 2006)? This information always seems to surprise my clients and colleagues. Voice hearing is far more common a phenomenon than one might believe! Voices (and/or visions) are often present in schizophrenia spectrum disorders, but also show up in other disorders like severe depression, bipolar disorder, neurological disorders, and substance use disorders and/or withdrawal. Within some cultures and religions, they are considered to be spiritual experiences (de Leede-Smith & Barkus, 2013; Roxburgh & Roe, 2014).

Psychotropic medications are commonly used by psychiatrists to treat clients' voices if and when these experiences impact their functioning (de Leede-Smith & Barkus; Penn, Meyer, Evans, Wirth, Cai, & Burchinal, 2009). Although antipsychotic medication reduces the frequency and severity of hallucinations in clients, researchers discovered that approximately 20–30% of clients with "treatment resistant" schizophrenia spectrum disorders continue to experience symptoms *despite* receiving high doses of antipsychotic medications with full medication compliance (Kane et al., 1988; Meltzer et al., 1990). Many of my clients who take antipsychotic medications continue to experience what I call "breakthrough experiences" and often discuss their fears about voices and visions returning. A couple of my clients who attend my Voices and Visions outpatient group make a weekly announcement, "my voices haven't returned yet" or "the voices aren't back, thank God!" Their lived experiences have taught them that their antipsychotic medications can serve as a barrier between them and their voices/visions. Unfortunately, sometimes the wall breaks or cracks, and pesky voices slip through. Sometimes antipsychotic medications (depending upon the client and the medication) can cause increased bouts of sleepiness, memory problems, drooling, weight gain, and/or make thoughts feel sluggish. These side effects can make one feel super self-conscious around friends, coworkers, family, and others. Recently, I was at a walk-a-thon for mental health awareness and was speaking with a fellow walker during the event. The woman, mid-conversation, stopped walking, spat on the side of the road, and sheepishly said, "I'm sorry, but my antipsychotic meds make me spit." I shrugged and said, "I get it—happened to me too." (Take it from someone who has been prescribed meds which made her drool—there is no stopping it. Even when I'd talk to people, the spit would build up in my mouth and it would need to go somewhere. I once tried to talk with a professor over the phone shortly after my hospitalization and kept having to spit (discreetly) into a paper napkin. Super classy, right?)

The physical side effects of various antipsychotic meds, in addition to the shame of voice hearing, made me feel very isolated socially. My clients also complain of similar feelings, and voice hearing is not something we like talking about in mixed company. As one of my clients who experiences command voices to graphically kill others explained, "How do you know who to trust when talking about these experiences?"

Researchers have also found that many clients with voices (even those who benefit from medication) continue to have problems with social functioning (Yildiz, Veznedaroglu, Eryavuz, & Kayahan, 2004). Even if the voices are well managed with meds, many folks with schizophrenia spectrum disorders struggle with low energy, lack of interest in activities, poor motivation, deficits of speech, decreased social awareness, and/or decreased emotional expressiveness. All these issues could impact one's ability to form and maintain friendships and romantic relationships.

Girl in the Crisis Unit Hallway

Recently, I was seeing clients at my clinic's inpatient crisis unit. The unit offers local folks a chance to be monitored as they detox from substances, to have their psychiatric medications adjusted in an observed environment, and/or to have a safe and contained environment while working with mental health providers to stabilize mental health symptoms.

As I walked down the hall to speak with a nurse, a young female client in her early twenties, Katie, walked (or I should say stomped) ahead of me, and appeared to be having a conversation with an invisible person. Her eyes appeared to be glazed over, her hair and clothes were disheveled, and she angrily yelled and cussed out an imaginary person in front of her. I watched staff ignore her, and I watched her glide in and out of the therapy group room engaged in her conversation. Over the next few days, Katie continued to stalk the halls, yelling and swearing, but was willing to talk with medical staff when they called upon her for vitals or a med check. Our crisis unit clinical director, who is well-versed in psychosis-related disorders, spoke with her daily, but staff largely left her alone. From an outsider point of view, she seemed isolated and lost in her own thoughts. I introduced myself to her and said, "Hi, I'm Andrea! I wanted to introduce myself and invite you to join my Voices and Visions outpatient group after you're discharged from this joint." Katie brightened and said, "I've heard about your group!" I went on to explain,

"I used to be a voice hearer and started this group for others who have similar experiences. Now they let me work here as a psychologist!" The client sat up straighter in her chair and said, "So there's hope? I can maybe even have a career?" I smiled and said, "There is always hope, and yes, maybe a career is in your future too. Come to group and we can discuss this stuff even further!" (That whole exchange made my entire week, and yes, this girl did end up coming to my group.)

Although I don't hear voices anymore (not since being hospitalized), I have compassion for this young client, and a strong conviction that folks struggling with voices need social engagement and social support as much as, if not more than, they need medication.

Groups for Clients with Auditory Verbal Hallucinations

When I was hospitalized for hearing voices, I was reluctant to talk to any medical staff about my voices, and I refused to tell any other client (even in a psych ward!) of my voice hearing experiences. Researchers also have found dealing with stigma and social withdrawal are some of the biggest challenges to recovery for those whose voices disrupt their functioning (Crawford, Killaspy, Kalaitzaki, Barrett, Byford et al., 2010). Don't get me wrong; fellow clients and I would talk about everything else under the sun during those long hours in the hospital, as I am a social butterfly. But my voices and visions, and all the meaning I made of them—off limits to everyone! I told the doctors and staff the barest of information because of the embarrassment I felt. After I was stabilized, I began to reflect upon the way I behaved while I was experiencing voices, and became even more embarrassed by the things I said and did. Being able to talk with fellow voice hearers about shared experiences would have been so helpful. Talking to a therapist, which, trust me, I did after being hospitalized, was challenging, because (as far as I knew) she did not have lived experience with voices. Apparently, researchers believed folks with voices could benefit from talking about their experiences as well, and they began exploring which psychosocial interventions could be most effective for working with clients who have auditory hallucinations.

One of the growing areas of research for voice hearers is group therapy (Ngo Nkouth, St-Onge, & Lepage, 2010; Penn, Meyer, Evans, Wirth, Cai, & Burchinal, 2009; Ruddle, Mason, & Wykes, 2011; Wykes, Steel, Everitt, & Tarrier, 2008). The research regarding groups for those whose voices disrupt their functioning shows this modality can be successful in reducing symptoms, decreasing distress, improving participants' beliefs about their psychosis-related experiences, and providing a sense of validation amongst group participants (Birchwood et al., 2011; Goodliffe, Hayward, Brown, Turton, & Dannahy, 2010; Hendry, 2011; Langer, Cangas, Salcedo, & Fuentes, 2012). Furthermore, group therapy for this client population is seen by health services as a way of maximizing resources and engaging clients who might not be appropriate for or interested in individual therapy (Ruddle, Mason, & Wykes, 2011).

There are a wide range of groups, which vary in content and structure: (1) unstructured, open-ended support; (2) problem-solving; (3) mindfulness; and (4) cognitive behavioral-therapy (CBT) (Ruddle, Mason, & Wykes, 2011). A great deal of quantitative research has been done demonstrating the efficacy of these various groups with clients who hear voices (Birchwood et al., 2011; Langer, Cangas, Salcedo, & Fuentes, 2012). A study by Langer, Cangas, Salcedo, and Fuentes (2012) explored the efficacy of a mindfulness-based cognitive behavioral-therapy group for clients with schizophrenia spectrum disorders. They randomly assigned 18 clients with psychosis to experimental and control groups. The experimental group received eight one-hour sessions of Mindfulness-Based Cognitive Therapy (MBCT). The control group was placed on the waitlist to receive MBCT. The researchers used three tools to measure client symptoms at the end of the study: the Clinical Global Impression Schizophrenia Scale (Haro, Kamath, & Ochoa, 2003), the Acceptance and Action Scale-II (Hayes, Strosahl, Wilson, Bissett, Pistorello, Toarmino, Polusny et al., 2004), and the Southampton

Mindfulness Questionnaire (Chadwick, Hember, Symes, Peters, Kuipers, & Dagnan, 2008). The experimental group scored significantly higher than the control group on their ability to respond mindfully to stressful internal events.

Another study by Penn, Meyer, Evans, Wirth, Cai, and Burchinal (2009) explored the efficacy of group "Cognitive Behavioral Therapy for the positive symptoms of psychosis" versus enhanced supportive therapy. The researchers used two assessment tools to measure main group outcomes: the Psychotic Symptom Rating Scales for auditory hallucinations (Haddock, McCarron, Tarrier, & Faragher, 1999), and the Belief about Voices Questionnaire-Revised (Chadwick, Lees, & Birchwood, 2000). Researchers also used additional tools as secondary outcome measures: the Positive and Negative Syndrome Scale (Kay, Fliszbein, & Opfer, 1987), the Social Functioning Scale (Birchwood, Smith, Cochrane, Wetton, & Copestake, 1990), the Beck Depression Inventory II (Beck, Steer, & Brown, 1996), the Rosenberg Self Esteem Scale (Rosenberg, 1965), and the Beck Cognitive Insight Scale (Beck, Baruch, Balter, Steer, & Warman, 2004). The group CBT condition was associated with a reduction in voices, visions, and unusual beliefs through a 12-month follow up. The supportive group condition showed a reduction in negative beliefs through a 12-month follow up.

There are at present only a few qualitative studies about groups for this client population that explore pathways to change: defining what "good outcomes" are and how these outcomes occur (Dillon & Hornstein, 2013; Lee, Hannan, Van Den Bosch, & Mouratoglou, 2002; Meddings, Walley, Collings, Tullett, McEwan, & Owen, 2011; Newton, Larkin, Melhuish, & Wykes, 2007; Ngo Nkouth, St-Onge, & Lepage, 2010; Webb, 2011). Newton, Larkin, Melhuish, and Wykes (2007) conducted a qualitative study which explored the experiences of group CBT with young people experiencing distressing auditory hallucinations. Eight participants, who completed a cognitive behavioral group intervention, were interviewed using a semi-structured interview. According to this research, "voices groups" were appreciated by these young people with auditory hallucinations as sources of therapy, support, and information.

In another qualitative study, Meddings, Walley, Collings, Tullett, McEwan, and Owen (2011) explored the efficacy of hearing voices support groups for clients with auditory hallucinations. Twelve group members took part in an in-depth evaluation. A triangulation of methodologies was used to collect data for this study. Outcome measures were completed prior to joining the group, after six months, and after 18 months. The outcome measures used were: the Scale of Voices Questionnaire (a series of Likert scale questions drawn from published scales) (Hustig & Hafner, 1990; Chadwick & Birchwood, 1995; Chadwick, Sambrooke, Rasch, & Davies, 2000), the Consumer Constructed Empowerment Scale (Rogers, Chamberlin, Langer Ellison, & Clean, 1997), Rosenberg's Self Esteem (Rosenberg, 1965), questions to determine group satisfaction, and the Personal Constructs Scale (Kelly, 1955). At the six-month point, group members each participated in a semi-structured interview. The outcome data was analyzed using SPSS. Themes emerged from the semi-structured interviews, were fed back to the group, and were used to inform discussions on how to improve the group. The group participants were very positive about the experience and found the group normalizing and de-stigmatizing. Group participants reported increases in self-esteem, and people's relationships with their voices improved. Unfortunately, these studies *all* appear to focus on the opinions of group members, which seems limited. The group members did not appear to mention decreases in positive symptoms (e.g., hearing voices), which is frequently measured by clinicians when they explore the efficacy of these types of groups (Penn, Meyer, Evans, Wirth, Cai, & Burchinal, 2009; Ruddle, Mason, & Wykes, 2011). There appears to be a discrepancy in the literature between what the group members find as a benefit from such groups versus what the clinical professionals hope to see as a benefit of such groups. This difference could result in misaligned treatment goals between clients and group leaders.

My Research Study

The discrepancy piqued my interest as both a clinician and someone with voice hearing experience. Consequently, I decided to explore the following research questions: (1) What do facilitators of groups for clients with psychosis-related experiences view as "positive group outcomes"?; (2) What factors and therapeutic interventions lead to positive group outcomes, per group facilitators? Specifically, my study explored what AVH group facilitators viewed as positive group outcomes and what process-related factors (e.g., therapist style, rapport, environment, therapeutic interventions) served to generate positive group outcomes. Since qualitative research methods emphasize process, they appeared best suited to study the research problem and questions identified in this study (Rossman & Rallis, 2012). Specifically, I utilized a case study approach, which allows for detailed explorations of a process, organization, individual, or group drawn from a class of similar phenomena.

Most case studies depict processes or perspectives as they unfold and often build an explanation for those events or outcomes (Rossman & Rallis, 2012). When there is more than one case, as with this study, the primary investigator conducts cross-case analyses for comparison purposes. Such analyses seek out commonalities across cases, as well as differences. The strength of case studies is in their ability to address practical problems (e.g., questions and situations, puzzling occurrences arising from daily practice) (Merriam, 1998). This is why a case study approach appeared appropriate for this exploration, for it addressed practical considerations of running groups for clients with AVH or other "psychosis"-related experiences (Rossman & Rallis, 2012).

Informed Consent

The group facilitators understood their participation in the research involved a one-off interview and completion of a demographic survey form. Confidentiality and its limits were explained in information sheets and explained verbally to participants over the phone. Research participants were also informed that all personal identifying information would be removed from all data, including written transcripts and any quotes used within the study.

Sampling and Sample Size

A non-random purposive sampling method was chosen for the study because potential subjects were invited based on a previously defined set of criteria reflecting relevant experience or expertise. Therefore, not everyone within the population theoretically represented by the samples had an equal chance of being selected for participation (Collins, Onwuegbuzie, & Jiao, 2006). In purposive samples, their size relies upon the concept of "saturation," or the point in the data collection process at which no new themes arise from the data (Creswell, 2007). Creswell (2007) and Guest, Bunce, and Johnson (2006) suggested a total sample size of anywhere from 6–30 participants is needed to reach data saturation using a grounded theory data analysis approach, which this study utilized. A total of ten participants were interviewed for this study. Two interviews were done through email because the interviewees felt their conversational English was not sufficient for a live interview.

Participants

Participants were recruited from postings on the United States and international listserv of The International Society for Psychological and Social Approaches to Psychosis. The researcher also met and recruited qualified participants at The International Society for Psychological and Social Approaches to Psychosis' March 2015 conference in New York, New York. Snowball sampling via email was also used to recruit participants and individuals who had published studies about facilitating AVH groups or had the necessary credentials to participate in this study. Qualified participants needed to meet the following criteria: (1) to be a licensed mental health worker (e.g., social worker, clinical counselor, psychiatrist, clinical psychologist) or a non-licensed "expert by experience" affiliated with The Hearing Voices Network (HVN), and (2) to have a minimum experience of six months facilitating a therapy group explicitly for clients who have "psychosis"-related experiences. The participants (five male and five female) ranged in age from 29 to 86 (mean age of 50.1 years). Table 2.1 contains additional demographic information of the group facilitators who participated in this study.

Materials

A semi-structured interview was used to obtain information from participants. This interview was between one and two hours in length and was conducted by the principal investigator. Some interviews were conducted via telephone and other interviews were conducted in person. Each interview was audio recorded and transcribed to guide the rest of the data collection process (Glaser & Straus, 1967).

According to Creswell (2006), member checking is often done at this stage to provide qualitative rigor to a study (Carlson, 2010). This process involves having the participants edit, clarify, or elaborate on the information they provided (Carlson, 2010). The participants were provided with a transcript of their interview approximately two to four weeks after the interview via email and were invited to edit, clarify, or elaborate on the information they provided, if they wished.

Data Analysis

This study used modified grounded theory, a strategy where likeness and differences among the data are recognized through coding and sorting transcripts into classifications (Rossman & Rallis, 2012). In addition, per Perry and Jensen (2001), modified grounded theory, unlike pure grounded theory, uses external dimensions, usually from the literature, in addition to theory building. Perry and Jensen (2001) contend that pure forms of grounded theory are diminished if the researcher maintains a professional naiveté (professional distance) until the study is completed. Per Perry and Jensen's (2001) description of modified

***Table 2.1* Demographic Information of Participants**

Facilitator's Country of Residence	*Facilitator's Race/ Ethnicity*	*Facilitator's Clinical License (if any)*	*Population with Whom Facilitator Works*	*Location of Group*	*Age Range of Clients with Whom Facilitator Works*	*Ethnicity of Clients*
United States	Caucasian	Social Worker	Urban	Community	18–65	Caucasian
United States	Caucasian	Licensed Clinical Counseling-Supervisor	Urban	Mental Health Agency	19–40s	Caucasian & African American
United States	Caucasian	Psychologist	Urban, Rural, Suburban	Forensic Hospital	18–70s	Variety of ethnicities
New Zealand	Caucasian	None	Urban	Forensic Hospital & Community	20–50	Maori, Caucasian, & African
Spain	Caucasian	Psychiatrist	Urban	Hospital	18–70s	Caucasian, Spanish Romanian, South American, & Arabian
United States	Caucasian	Psychologist	Suburban	Community	20s–40s	African American & Caucasian
England	Caucasian	Psychologist	Urban & Suburban	Mental Health Agency	18–65	Eastern European, Indian, Iranian, British, Irish, African, and Afro-Caribbean
Israel	Jewish	Psychiatrist	Urban	Hospital	"Adult"	Jewish
United States	Caucasian	None	Urban	Mental Health Agency and Community	20s & 50s–60s	African American & Caucasian
United States	Caucasian	Psychologist	Urban	Forensic Mental Health Ward	18–65	Hispanic, African American, & Caucasian

grounded theory, I approached this study with my own preconceived ideas, grounded in the literature, about what data might be revealed/uncovered, *in addition* to the theory building based upon the data collected.

Coding

Within data-driven coding, two types of coding take place: open coding followed by closed coding (Charmaz, 2001). The data analysis process went as follows:

- The open coding portion involved a close reading of each participants' transcript at least twice and a code word or phrase was created and assigned to each data unit (e.g., paragraph or sentence) (DeCuir-Gunby, Marshall, & McCulloch, 2010).
- The language of the code assigned to each data unit was kept as close to the participants' own words and phrasing as possible to retain each facilitator's quirks, idiosyncrasies, and peculiarities.

The main goal of this particular process was to capture the various codes which emerged from the interviews, and each participant's interview yielded multiple codes (DeCuir-Gunby, Marshall, & McCulloch, 2010; Field, 2014). The final step was to determine the reliability and utility of the codes (DeCuir-Gunby, Marshall, & McCulloch, 2010).

Translating Into Themes

Themes pull together a lot of data into more meaningful units; it is a way of grouping initial codes into a parsimonious collection of ideas (Cruzes & Dyba, 2011). I generated a thematic tree to help sort the codes into themes. Throughout this process, I discussed my theme creation with my dissertation chair, Dr. Sears, and qualitative consultant, Dr. Becker-Klein. Ultimately, the aim was to use the themes to help me to identify what my participants viewed as (1) the mechanisms of change for AVH groups and (2) what they viewed as good group outcomes for AVH groups (Cruzes & Dyba, 2011). I also searched for alternative explanations for the data, keeping the following questions in mind: "But why is this technique, characteristic, training, etc. good for clients who attend AVH groups? Why with this population?" Additionally, I returned to the current literature on AVH groups to see if relevant theories proposed by other researchers extended, contradicted, or deepened my interpretations. I discovered my findings were well supported by the current literature (Rossman & Rallis, 2012). However, my findings add new data because few researchers have explored what *AVH facilitators* view as good outcomes and mechanisms of change (Dillon & Hornstein, 2013; Jones, Marino, & Hansen, 2015).

Based upon what the facilitators said, six master themes were generated, which form the basis of the following chapters in this book. The quotations used in each chapter were selected based upon their representativeness of that particular theme.

The experience of conducting this research, talking to group facilitators from around the world, and now writing about my lived experience in a very public way has been empowering and healing. I see the fruits of my research labors pay off weekly in the Voices and Visions group (V&V group) I have been facilitating for the past two years. I work in community mental health, and resources are tightly allocated. Therefore, if group membership was too small, my V&V group would quickly be shut down by management. That's just the way business, including the mental health business, can be sometimes. Other groups have come and gone—ones which seemed like popular concepts, such as Anger Management or Relationships Issues. I believe having one foot in both camps (woman with lived experience and clinician, armed with research and familiar with psychosis) helped contribute to the group's ongoing success. Therefore, in the subsequent chapters I will share what I know about running groups for voice hearers, insider info about groups from a former voice hearer (me), and what my fellow facilitators shared about running groups for this population. My hope is that this book inspires you to learn more about running groups for voice hearers, develop a group of your own, and work with folks who have extreme state experiences (e.g., hallucinations and delusions).

Over the years, and throughout this book, I have chosen to call psychosis-related symptoms "extreme state experiences," as many in the Hearing Voices Network do, because this description is less pathologizing and better matches what clients are going through. However, some clients prefer to call their experiences by traditional psychological terms. It's a personal preference—and when in doubt, ask the client their preference!

Summary Points

- Psychotropic medication can come with some negative side effects and can serve as a barrier between the voices/visions and the client. However, at times, even clients being effectively treated with medication can have "breakthrough" experiences.
- Group therapy for those who hear voices is emerging as a helpful tool and one that is being researched more as a treatment alternative. Despite its emergence as a therapeutic tool, there appear to be discrepancies between group leaders and group members as to what makes groups for voice hearers most effective.
- The remaining chapters of this book discuss the themes that emerged as a result of a novel research study that sought to explore what group facilitators view as positive group outcomes and what factors and therapeutic interventions lead to these positive group experiences. The six main themes will be described in the following chapters.

References

Beck, A. T., Baruch, E., Balter, J. M., Steer, R. A., & Warman, D. M. (2004). A new instrument for measuring insight: The Beck Cognitive Insight Scale. *Schizophrenia Research, 68*(2), 319–329.

Beck, A. T., Steer, R. A., & Brown, G. K. (1996). *Beck depression inventory*. San Antonio, TX: The psychological corporation.

Birchwood, M., Peters, E., Tarrier, N., Dunn, G., Lewis, S., Wykes, T., & … Michail, M. (2011). A multi-centre, randomised controlled trial of cognitive therapy to prevent harmful compliance with command hallucinations. *BMC Psychiatry, 11*(853–859).

Birchwood, M., Smith, J. O., Cochrane, R., Wetton, S., & Copestake, S. O. N. J. A. (1990). The Social Functioning Scale. The development and validation of a new scale of social adjustment for use in family intervention programmes with schizophrenic patients. *The British Journal of Psychiatry, 157*(6), 853–859.

Carlson, J. A. (2010). Avoiding Traps in Member Checking. *The Qualitative Report, 15*(5), 1102–1113. Retrieved from https://nsuworks.nova.edu/tqr/vol15/iss5/4.

Chadwick, P., & Birchwood, M. (1995). The omnipotence of voices. II: The Beliefs About Voices Questionnaire (BAVQ). *The British Journal of Psychiatry, 166*(6), 773–776.

Chadwick, P., Hember, M., Symes, J., Peters, E., Kuipers, E., & Dagnan, D. (2008). Responding mindfully to unpleasant thoughts and images: Reliability and validity of the Southampton mindfulness questionnaire (SMQ). *British Journal of Clinical Psychology, 47*(4), 451–455.

Chadwick, P., Lees, S., & Birchwood, M. A. X. (2000). The revised beliefs about voices questionnaire (BAVQ-R). *The British Journal of Psychiatry, 177*(3), 229–232.

Chadwick, P., Sambrooke, S., Rasch, S., & Davies, E. (2000). Challenging the omnipotence of voices: Group cognitive behavior therapy for voices. *Behaviour Research and Therapy, 38*(10), 993–1003.

Charmaz, K. (2001). Qualitative interviewing and grounded theory analysis. In J. F. Gubrium & J. A. Holstein (Eds.), *Handbook of interview research: Context and method* (pp. 675–694). Thousand Oaks, CA: Sage.

Collins, K., Onwuegbuzie, A., & Jiao, Q. (2006). Prevalence of mixed methods sampling designs in social science research. *Evaluation and Research in Education, 19*(2), 83–101.

Crawford, M. J., Killaspy, H., Kalaitzaki, E., Barrett, B., Byford, S., Patterson, S., & Waller, D. (2010). The MATISSE study: A randomized trial of group art therapy for people with schizophrenia. *BMC Psychiatry, 10*(65), 1–9.

Creswell, J. W. (2007). *Qualitative inquiry and research design: Choosing among five traditions* (2nd ed.). Thousand Oaks, CA: Sage.

Cruzes, D. S., & Dyba, T. (2011, September). Recommended steps for thematic synthesis in software engineering. In *Empirical Software Engineering and Measurement (ESEM), 2011 International Symposium on* (pp. 275–284). IEEE.

DeCuir-Gunby, J. T., Marshall, P. L., & McCulloch, A. W. (2010). Developing and using a codebook for the analysis of interview data: An example from a professional development research project. *Field Methods, 23*(2), 136–155.

de Leede-Smith, S. & Barkus, E. (2013). A comprehensive review of auditory verbal hallucinations: Lifetime prevalence, correlates, mechanisms in healthy and clinical individuals. *Frontiers in Human Neuroscience, 7*, 1–25.

Dillon, J., & Hornstein, G. A. (2013). Hearing voices peer support groups: A powerful alternative for people in distress. *Psychosis, 5*(3), 286–295.

Field, Julia E. (2014). From Goal-Striving to "Right Intention": A Grounded Theory Analysis of Interviews with Mindfulness-Based Stress Reduction Participants. In *BSU Honors Program Theses and Projects*. Item 34.

Glaser, B., & Straus, A. (1967). *The discovery of grounded theory*. Chicago: Aldine.

Goodliffe, L., Hayward, M., Brown, D., Turton, W., & Dannahy, L. (2010). Group person-based cognitive therapy for distressing voices: Views from the hearers. *Psychotherapy Research, 20*(4), 447–461.

Guest, G., Bunce, A., & Johnson, L. (2006). How many interviews are enough: An experiment with data saturation and variability. *Field Methods, 18*(1), 59–82.

Haddock, G., McCarron, J., Tarrier, N., & Faragher, E. B. (1999). Scales to measure dimensions of hallucinations and delusions: The psychotic symptom rating scales (PSYRATS). *Psychological Medicine, 29*(4), 879–889.

Haro, J. M., Kamath, S. A., Ochoa, S., Novick, D., Rele, K., Fargas, A., & ... Jones, P. B. (2003) The Clinical Global Impression–Schizophrenia scale: a simple instrument to measure the diversity of symptoms present in schizophrenia. *Acta Psychiatrica Scandinavica, 107*, 16–23.

Hayes, S. C., Strosahl, K. D., Wilson, K. G., Bissett, R. T., Pistorello, J., Taormino, D., & ... McCurry, S. M. (2004). Measuring experiential avoidance: A preliminary test of a working model. *Psychological Record, 54*, 553–578.

Hendry, G. L. (2011). *What are the experiences of those attending a self-help hearing voices group: An interpretive phenomenological approach*. University of Leeds.

Hustig, H. H., & Hafner, R. J. (1990). Persistent auditory hallucinations and their relationship to delusions and mood. *The Journal of Nervous and Mental Disease, 178*(4), 264–267.

Johns, L. C., Cannon, M., Singleton, N., Murray, R. M., Farrell, M., Brugha, T., & ... Meltzer, H. (2004). Prevalence and correlates of self-reported psychotic symptoms in the British population. *The British Journal of Psychiatry, 185*, 298–305.

Jones, N., Marino, C., & Hansen, M. (2015). The Hearing Voices Movement in United States: Findings from a national survey of group. *Psychosis, 8*(2), 106–117.

Kane, J., Honigfeld, G., Singer, J., & Meltzer, H. (1988). Clozapine for the treatment-resistant schizophrenic: A double comparison with chlorpromazine. *Archives of General Psychiatry, 45*(9), 789.

Kay, S. R., Fliszbein, A., & Opfer, L. A. (1987). The positive and negative syndrome scale (PANSS) for schizophrenia. *Schizophrenia Bulletin, 13*(2), 261.

Kelly, G. A. (1955). *The psychology of personal constructs, vols. 1 and 2.* New York: Norton (reprinted by Routledge, 1991).

Langer, Á. I., Cangas, A. J., Salcedo, E., & Fuentes, B. (2012). Applying mindfulness therapy in a group of psychotic individuals: A controlled study. *Behavioural and Cognitive Psychotherapy, 40*(1), 105–109.

Lee, K., Hannan, C., Van Den Bosch, J., Williams, J., & Mouratoglou, V. (2002). Evaluating a hearing voices group for older people: Preliminary findings. *International Journal of Geriatric Psychiatry, 17*(11), 1079–1080.

Meddings, S., Walley, L., Collings, T., Tullett, F., McEwan, B., & Owen, K. (2011). Are hearing voices groups effective? A preliminary evaluation. *Journal of Psychiatric & Mental Health Nursing, 7,* 135–141.

Meltzer, H. (1992). Treatment of the neuroleptic-non-responsive schizophrenic patient. *Schizophrenia Bulletin, 18*(3), 515–542.

Merriam, S. B. (1998). *Qualitative research and case study applications in education* (Rev. ed.). San Francisco: Jossey-Bass.

Newton, E., Larkin, M., Melhuish, R., & Wykes, T. (2007). More than just a place to talk: Young people's experiences of group psychological therapy as an early intervention for auditory hallucinations. *Psychology & Psychotherapy: Theory, Research & Practice, 80*(1), 127–149.

Ngo Nkouth, B., St-Onge, M., & Lepage, S. (2010). The group as a place of training and universality of the experience of voice hearers. *Groupwork: An Interdisciplinary Journal for Working With Groups, 20*(2), 45–64.

Penn, D. L., Meyer, P. S., Evans, E., Wirth, R. J., Cai, K., & Burchinal, M. (2009). A randomized controlled trial of group cognitive-behavioral therapy vs. enhanced supportive therapy for auditory hallucinations. *Schizophrenia Research, 109*(1–3), 52–59.

Perry, C. and Jensen, O. (2001). Approaches to combining induction and deduction in one research study, ANZMAC 2001, Auckland, New Zealand, December. 130.195.95.71:8081/WWW/ANZMAC2001/anzmac/AUTHORS/pdfs/Perry1.pdf, 9.10.2004.

Rogers, E. S., Chamberlin, J., Langer Ellison, M., & Clean, T. (1997). A consumer constructed scale to measure empowerment among users of mental health services. *Psychiatric Services, 48*(8), 1042–1047.

Rosenberg, M. (1965). *Society and the adolescent self-image.* Princeton, NJ: Princeton University Press.

Rossman, G. B., & Rallis, S. F. (2012). *Learning in the field: An introduction to qualitative research.* Amherst, MA: Sage.

Roxburgh, E. C., & Roe, C. A. (2014). Reframing voices and visions using a spiritual model. An interpretative phenomenological analysis of anomalous experiences in mediumship. *Mental Health, Religion, & Culture, 17*(6), 641–653.

Ruddle, A., Mason, O., & Wykes, T. (2011). A review of hearing voices groups: Evidence and mechanisms of change. *Clinical Psychology Review, 31*(5), 757–766.

Scott, J., Chant, D., Andrews, G., & McGrath, J. (2006). Psychotic-like experiences in the general community: the correlates of CIDI psychosis screen items in an Australian sample. *Psychological Medicine, 36*(2), 231–238.

Webb, J. (2011). *Hearing voices: Coping, resilience and recovery*. University of Leeds.

Wykes, T., Steel, C., Everitt, B., & Tarrier, N. (2008). Cognitive behavior therapy for schizophrenia: effect sizes, clinical models, and methodological rigor. *Schizophrenia Bulletin, 34*(3), 523–537.

Yildiz, M., Veznedaroglu, B., Eryavuz, A., & Kayahan, B. (2004). Psychosocial skills training on social functioning and quality of life in the treatment of schizophrenia: A controlled study in Turkey. *International Journal of Psychiatry in Clinical Practice, 8*, 219–225.

3

ESSENTIAL COMPONENTS

What Makes a Group for Voice Hearers Effective?

> *Reflection: Prior to reading this chapter, what do you know about treatment of voice hearing? How would you know if your group is effective?*

When I first learned about hearing voices groups, the concept seemed both novel and obvious to me (as a former voice hearer) at the same time. Creating groups which promote growth, recovery, and an open dialogue about voice hearing (often facilitated by voice hearers) seemed like a fantastic idea to me. When involved with developing a hearing voices group for the community mental health agency in which we worked, fellow colleagues and I first had to consider: What are reasonable and positive group outcomes or goals for such groups? At the time, we had difficulty finding relevant research, and came across only limited helpful resources. We found articles outlining first person accounts of how voice hearers viewed groups, the Hearing Voices Network (very helpful), and articles about Cognitive Behavioral Therapy for Psychosis (CBTp). The difficulties we experienced in finding resources inspired me to talk with group facilitators who were working within their communities (not just those conducting research) to learn from them what worked and what was not effective. What did these facilitators consider good group outcomes, and how did they achieve them?

As I spoke with different expert facilitators who did individual and group therapy for voice hearers, I was surprised by the diversity in theoretical frameworks from which they worked. I'm not going to promote one theoretical orientation over the others, because I have seen the effectiveness of a number of different approaches. As a psychologist who runs hearing voices groups and supervises other group facilitators, I have discovered that theoretical approaches are only as good as the skill of the facilitator using them. Some group facilitators are masterful in their use of theory, whereas the same theory in the hands of a less skilled clinician can fall flat. However, I think it will be helpful to provide an overview of the most common group facilitation approaches for voice hearers (e.g., Acceptance and Commitment Therapy, CBTp, hybrid Hearing Voices/CBTp).

Cognitive Behavioral Group Therapy for Psychosis

Researchers found group therapy tailored to voice hearers could be quite effective in helping this population manage their symptoms—even after psychotropic medications have failed (Ruddle, Mason, & Wykes, 2011). CBT for psychosis is the most widely researched and well-known treatment approach for working with clients who have experienced both positive and negative psychosis-related symptoms. This approach was recommended as an adjunctive therapy to antipsychotic medication by the American Psychiatric Association (APA) treatment guidelines and the United Kingdom's National Institute for Health and Care Excellence (NICE, Kuipers, Yesufu-Udechuku, Taylor, & Kendall, 2014).

Cognitive Behavioral Therapy for Psychosis is a formulation-driven treatment which focuses on decreasing distress related to a client's beliefs/appraisal of their voices, visions, and unusual beliefs (Morrison, Renton, Dunn, Williams, & Bentall, 2004; Kingdon & Turkington, 2005; Beck, Rector, Stolar, & Grant, 2009). Studies by a number of researchers have found group CBT for auditory hallucinations to be more effective than "treatment as usual" (antipsychotic medication, case management, access to drop-in centers), supportive therapy, or wait lists (Barrowclough et al., 2006; Bechdolf et al., 2010; Lecomte, Leclerc, & Wykes, 2012; Penn et al., 2009; Peters et al., 2010; Wykes, Steel, Everitt,

& Tarrier, 2008). For example, Penn et al. (2009) conducted a study (N = 62) in which they examined group CBT for auditory hallucinations versus an active control treatment (e.g., enhanced supportive therapy). The group CBT for auditory hallucinations was a manual-based treatment comprised of 12 one-hour weekly sessions based on the work of Wykes and colleagues (Wykes et al., 1999). Sessions covered a variety of topics: psychoeducation, content of auditory hallucinations, behavioral analyses of auditory hallucinations, identifying situations which increase or decrease auditory hallucinations, and coping skills for auditory hallucinations. The enhanced supportive therapy group (ST) used a 12-week manual-based intervention whose primary goal was to improve social integration into the community. ST focused on establishing a therapeutic alliance, agreeing on interpersonal goals, and social integration. Therefore, unlike CBT, group leaders provided direct advice and incorporated suggestions from group members.

Participants were assessed at baseline, post-treatment, three months, and 12 months on the following measures of mood, self-esteem, insight, social functioning, and hospitalizations: the Psychotic Symptom Rating Scales for auditory hallucinations (Haddock, McCarron, Tarrier, & Faragher, 1999), the Beliefs About Voices Questionnaire Revised (Chadwick, Lees, & Birchwood, 2000), the Social Functioning Scale (Birchwood, Smith, Cochrane, Wetton, & Copestake, 1990), the Beck Depression Inventory-II (Beck, Steer, & Brown, 1996), the Rosenberg Stability of Self Scale (RSSS, Rosenberg, 1965), and the Beck Cognitive Insight Scale (Beck, Baruch, Balter, Steer, & Warman, 2004). The researchers found that group CBT was associated with lower general and total symptoms scores on the Positive and Negative Syndrome Scale (PANNS, Kay, Fiszbein, & Opler, 1987) through a 12-month follow-up, relative to those who received group ST. Overall, the outcomes for participants improved in both therapy groups. The ST group had a specific impact on the auditory hallucinations, and the group CBT had more of an impact on general psychotic symptoms.

Wykes, Steel, Everitt, and Tarrier (2008) conducted a meta-analysis of 34 studies that explored the efficacy of CBT for psychosis (CBTp) versus a "treatment as usual" group (TAU) (e.g., medication, case management) or a control adjunct treatment that was considered inactive for the main outcome. The researchers used the Clinical Trial Assessment Measure (CTAM) to analyze the various studies. Overall, the researchers found that Cognitive Behavioral Therapy for Psychosis (CBTp) had a beneficial effect on positive symptoms (e.g., delusions, hallucinations, and disordered speech). These researchers also found that psychological treatment trials which made no attempt to mask the group allocation were likely to have inflated effect sizes.

More recently, studies have shifted focus to CBT that specifically addresses distressing voices (CBTv, Thomas et al., 2014; Lincoln & Peters, 2018) rather than the broader symptom approach of CBTp. The CBTv approach believes it is not the experience of voice hearing which brings distress but rather clients' beliefs about the power and meaning of their voices which cause upset (Hazell et al., 2018). This approach focuses on normalizing voice hearing, using behavioral experiments to test unhelpful beliefs about voices, improving clients' capacity to cope with their voices, developing improved emotional regulation strategies for voice management, and revising negative beliefs about the self.

As someone with lived experience, I appreciate an approach that addresses the distress about beliefs regarding my voices. When a voice or voices showed up, I wasn't bothered by its presence per se, but felt confused by how disruptive these voices were to my belief system. I experienced command voices telling me to harm myself (e.g., stab myself in the eye), but prior to hearing these voices, I had never entertained the idea of self-harm. I would perseverate on why I was being told to self-harm. Why now? Why my eyeball? (Ugh—I felt squeamish then when I heard it, and I shudder even now.) Voices would tell me I was being chased while I drove my car, and told me I had to find safety. I already felt unsafe (I had concurrent PTSD symptoms at the time), so these voices seemed to reinforce my feelings that the world was unsafe.

Acceptance and Commitment Therapy for Voice Hearing

More recently, research is emerging about the application of Acceptance and Commitment Therapy (ACT) with clients who experience voices (Bacon, Farhall, & Fossey, 2014; Louise, Fitzpatrick, Strauss, Rossell, & Thomas, 2018; Shawyer, Farhall, Thomas, & Hayes, 2017). ACT attempts to modify *the relationship* one has with negative private events (e.g., such as thoughts and feelings) versus the content or presence of these events (Hayes, Strosahl, & Wilson, 1999). These changes are achieved by increasing psychological flexibility in order to develop meaningful steps towards chosen life values (Morris, Johns, & Oliver, 2013). Psychological flexibility or cognitive shift responses include acceptance, mindful awareness, defusion, and values-based behavioral activation. This approach is in contrast to managing distress through suppression of distressing experiences, or by behavioral and emotional avoidance of upsetting negative private events (Morris, Johns, & Oliver, 2013).

Butler et al. (2016) conducted a qualitative study exploring the use of Acceptance and Commitment Therapy for psychosis (ACTp) with therapy groups. The researchers hoped to help clients engage in activities which fostered personal meaning and to increase their ability to better relate to distressing psychosis-related symptoms rather than attempting to reduce or eliminate them (Butler et al., 2016). The researchers ran four groups that lasted two hours each and additionally ran two "booster" sessions which were held eight weeks after the group program was completed. Before the series of four groups began, researchers ran a "taster" session, which introduced interested participants to ACT ideas. Participants were then invited to opt into the group series. Researchers found that this helped with retention of subjects.

Participants were recruited from adult community psychosis services. Two separate studies were conducted, 33 separate groups were run, and 120 participants received a group ACTp intervention. An important ACTp intervention is based upon the "Passengers on the Bus" Metaphor (Harris, 2009) and was used throughout the four group therapy sessions. The metaphor illustrates being on a "bus of life," where the bus driver makes choices which steers the bus towards or away from certain values. On the bus, various passengers represent thoughts, feelings, or memories, and how the driver interacts with these "passengers" limits or increases movement towards values (Butler et al., 2016). The groups followed a similar format: (1) a warm-up exercise, (2) two noticing (mindfulness) exercises, (3) discussion of out-of-session activity from the previous week, (4) group discussion/activity, and (5) planning an out-of-session activity for the coming week (Butler et al., 2016). Based on this group research, along with data from other trials of ACTp group therapy (Johns et al., 2015), the researchers concluded that this therapeutic approach is effective for individuals with psychosis-related symptoms. ACTp increases client well-being and helps them better choose values-based courses of action (Butler et al., 2016).

From a lived experience perspective, the ACTp idea about modifying the relationship with one's voices makes so much intuitive sense. Voice hearers have relationships with their voices—some good and some bad—but these relationships are as fraught with stress and joy as those we have with family and friends. There was a part of me which missed the voices when they left, for they often made me laugh when I was scared in the hospital. Some of the voices were awful, and their commands made no sense, much like an abusive family member or partner. I developed a mindfulness practice years earlier in order to combat my PTSD symptoms after hearing about the benefits from clients and colleagues. This practice taught me to not be fused with my thoughts and decreased my emotional reactivity. In learning to have better emotional control, I was able to explore the meaning of the voices I heard and to develop a healthier (less reactive) understanding of them.

Mechanisms of Change with Group Therapy for Hallucinations

While these studies supported the effectiveness of various types of groups for this client population, few of the quantitative studies to date have explored the mechanisms of change in detail (e.g., specifics of interventions used, the environment where the groups were held, therapist characteristics, rapport). Fortunately, a handful of studies have emerged that have focused on mechanisms of change for this type of population and group treatment modality (Hendry, 2011; Lee, Hannan, Van Den Bosch, Williams, & Mouratoglou, 2002; Meddings et al., 2004; Ruddle, Mason, & Wykes, 2011; Webb, 2011). Hendry (2011) explored the experiences of those attending a support group in the UK. Three main research questions were asked by the author: (a) Why do participants attend the Hearing Voices Group?; (b) What do participants enjoy about attending the Hearing Voices Group?; and (c) What do participants find unhelpful about attending the Hearing Voices Group?. A convenience sample of seven adults was recruited, and participants were interviewed using a semi-structured interview schedule. A phenomenological analysis was conducted for individual participants, and then a group analysis was conducted across participants to identify master themes and sub-themes. The six master themes were: threats to engagement, catalyst for change, coming together to help ourselves, vicarious emotional experience, a secure base, and belonging to a special tribe. Hendry's (2011) research added to the existing knowledge base by exploring how participants developed attachments to the group and its members.

In a similar study, Lee, Hannan, Van Den Bosch, Williams, and Mouratoglou (2002) examined whether a support group would be useful in reducing the distress experienced by older voice hearers. They hypothesized that the psychological distress experienced as a result of hearing voices would be reduced by group participation, thus helping people to feel more powerful in relation to their voice(s). The group met for an hour over 12 weeks and had five group members. Quantitative data were collected using the following measures: the Hospital Anxiety and Depression Scale (Zigmand & Snaith, 1983), the Rosenberg Stability of Self Scale (RSSS, Rosenberg, 1965), the Auditory Hallucination Rating Scale, and the Revised Beliefs About Voices Questionnaire (Chadwick, Lees, & Birchwood, 2000). Qualitative data was collected using a semi-structured interview. Overall, participants reported they found the normalization of being around other voice hearers helpful, and they appreciated the opportunity to discuss the social stigma associated with hearing voices.

Meddings et al. (2004) conducted a mixed methods study aimed to measure the efficacy of a Hearing Voices Group (HVG). The evaluation included broader conceptions regarding outcomes, and a qualitative element to its enquiry. The quantitative data was collected using the following outcome measures: Scale of Voices Questionnaire (a series of Likert scale questions drawn from published scales) (Hustig & Hafner, 1990; Chadwick & Birchwood, 1995; Chadwick, Sambrooke, Rasch, & Davies, 2000), Consumer Constructed Empowerment Scales (Sciarappa, Rogers & Chamberlin, 1994), a Personal Constructs Scale (Kelly, 1955), and Rosenberg's Stability of Self Scale (RSSS, Rosenberg, 1965). Participants were also asked to determine group satisfaction, and these were anchored using a 1–7 Likert scale. This study found that after attending the HVG, members' hospital bed use decreased. Group members used far more coping strategies and were able to talk to far more people about their voices after attending the group. They reported feeling more empowered, less stigmatized, and less alone. Finally, more people reported getting involved with work, volunteering, or school. After attending the group, self-esteem increased, as measured by Rosenberg's Stability of Self Scale (RSSS, Rosenberg, 1965; Meddings et al., 2004). Themes from the qualitative interviews highlighted the value that participants placed on group processes: universality, instillation of hope, self-disclosure, mutual support, and improved social functioning (Meddings et al., 2004).

Finally, a qualitative study by Webb (2011) sought to understand individual voice hearer's experiences of support from group therapy, and how a client's participation in group is linked to their experiences of coping, resilience, and recovery. Specifically, the purpose was to answer the following two questions: (1) What was the experience of support you have received in relation to hearing voices?; and, (2) How has this support influenced your coping, resilience, and recovery? Seven individuals who heard voices were recruited from a local hearing voices group and were given a semi-structured interview. Whether support was perceived as helpful or unhelpful was linked to specific factors the interviewees considered influential in their process of recovery. These included being in a safe and non-judgmental environment, being offered hope and validation of their experiences, and having a means to socially connect and empower their position so they could be more active in their own recovery. The researcher suggested a need for more training in the conceptual frameworks and models of recovery, a greater focus on working with the family and wider support, enhanced collaborative working alliances, and more tailored outcome measures to better meet these individuals' needs during the recovery process.

Facilitators' Opinions Regarding Effective AVH Groups

A study by Jones, Marino, and Hansen (2015) explored the hearing voices group facilitators' perspectives regarding group membership, clinician involvement, perceived impact on participants, and facilitator training. They uncovered three significant areas of interest: (1) disagreements or uncertainty about whether to keep the focus of HVGs to strictly "hallucinations" or to include individuals who have other "extreme state" related experiences, such as unusual beliefs and dissociative states; (2) tension regarding HVG collaboration with licensed clinicians, because many facilitators surveyed wanted to avoid the over-clinicalization of HVGs; and (3) facilitators' insights into the impact of these groups on participants, specifically the "centrality of trauma and the exploration of links between voices and trauma" (Jones, Marino, & Hansen, 2015, p. 10).

Additionally, Dillon and Hornstein (2013) wrote a paper explaining the structure of HVGs, the importance of facilitator training, and principles related to the Hearing Voices Network, which does a great deal of training, advocacy, and support for participants and facilitators of HVGs. They indicated HVGs are not tightly structured and are intended to help voice hearers better communicate and understand their individual experiences; the importance of allowing clients to have agency (e.g., not telling clients what to do), empowering clients to challenge the stigmatizing labels they receive from others such as peers, mental health professionals, and family members; and the importance of acceptance, respect, and validation. Dillon and Hornstein (2013) also explored the facilitation skills necessary to effectively run an HVG, such as to not step in as an "expert," but to encourage group members to make decisions regarding the group's activities, direction, structure, procedural changes, etc. They indicated facilitators should receive training if they choose to run such HVGs, such as workshops available through the Hearing Voices Network, because this encourages facilitators to see recovery is possible, and prevents facilitators from inadvertently harming group members. Dillon and Hornstein (2013) also stressed the importance of facilitators to be non-judgmental and to cultivate self-awareness so that they are better equipped to sit with the difficult feelings that clients discuss and explore in group, such as anxiety, fear, anger, and sadness.

Other Therapeutic Factors Contributing to Good Group Outcomes

Unfortunately, researchers have yet to systematically explore other important factors which might contribute to "good group outcomes" for AVH groups, such as the group room environment. A study by Ozerengin and Cowen (1974) found that the noise level of the hospital environment influenced the behavior of clients with schizophrenia. Thirty clients with schizophrenia were chosen by researchers. Fifteen were chosen for the "withdrawn group," who displayed symptoms such as social withdrawal behavior, verbalizations, and conceptual disorganization. Another 15 participants were chosen for the "active group," who displayed symptoms such as psychomotor agitation, anxiety, and conceptual organization. Initially, the participants were placed in a quiet environment for three hours over a six-week period, where the noise level was kept between 40–60 decibels. At the end of six weeks, the same set of participants was placed in a noisy environment where the noise level was kept between 80–90 decibels for the same period of time. Each participant was administered the Detroit Tests of Learning Aptitude (digit span and motor perception tests, Baker & Leland, 1959) at the beginning and end of the testing periods. In addition, each participant's motor, activity, and verbal productivity was rated every morning and afternoon using a rating scale. Finally, every subject in the study, as well as 100 other patients in the building, were evaluated in terms of medication requirements and adjustments by an independent psychiatrist who was blind to what individuals were part of the study. In the noisy environment, the active group's test performance decreased, and their conceptual disorganization, anxiety, and restlessness grew. However, placing the withdrawn group in the noisy environment had a positive effect. In the quiet environment, the withdrawn group showed considerable regression—they were more withdrawn and experienced more conceptual disorganization. In the quiet environment, the active group showed more conceptual organization, improved test performance, decreased anxiety, and increased motor and verbal productivity.

Other therapist factors, such as rapport, personality, and style, may also influence "good group outcomes." According to multiple researchers, good therapist/client rapport facilitates good communication and may also improve achievement of expected treatment outcomes (Leach, 2005; Paley & Lawton, 2001). Yalom and Leszcz (2005) state that a good therapeutic relationship with group members leads to better group outcomes. Unfortunately, there does not appear to be any research to date that directly explores therapeutic rapport with clients with AVH.

Differing Points of View Between Clients and Facilitators?

Thus far, these various qualitative studies explored what clients believed to be good outcomes. Limited data exists regarding what the group leaders believe to be positive outcomes, aside from the papers by a handful of researchers (Dillon & Hornstein, 2013; Jones, Marino, & Hansen, 2015). These insights were generated from individuals exclusively connected with the Hearing Voices Network, and predominantly United States HVN affiliated facilitators. What about facilitators from other countries, or group leaders not affiliated with the HVN? Additionally, neither set of authors delves into tremendous detail regarding what facilitators believe to be the mechanisms of change for HVGs and what they view as good group outcomes. What if the facilitators' beliefs regarding mechanisms of change and outcomes differ from the clients'? These different expectations could cause client frustration and facilitator dissatisfaction. Yalom and Leszcz (2005) point out that although they do not directly influence group outcomes, the group facilitators' influence is present in the group room.

Having a dual perspective of being a voice hearer and a group facilitator led me to wonder how group facilitators of AVH groups (both affiliated and not affiliated with the HVN) view their groups, the clients, treatment goals, and intervention techniques. Do they view their work through the multiple lenses of hope, playfulness, connection, and agency like I do? What do group facilitators of AVH groups from all over the world believe are useful outcomes, and how do they go about achieving them? These questions were the motivating force that led to my research and to the writing of this book.

Summary Points

- There are many different theoretical frameworks for Hearing Voices groups and they all require a skilled leader.

- Many studies have demonstrated efficacy of group treatment, based on various types of groups. In group therapy in general, it appears that good rapport between group leaders and group members is a helpful component, however this has not been directly studied with the hearing voices population.
- There is no universal agreement on what constitutes a successful outcome for Hearing Voices groups, however participants often report that they enjoy the normalization of being around other voice hearers and they appreciate the opportunity to discuss the social stigma associated with hearing voices.

References

Bacon, T., Farhall, J., & Fossey, E. (2014). The active therapeutic processes of acceptance and commitment therapy for persistent symptoms of psychosis: Clients' perspectives. *Behavioural & Cognitive Psychotherapy, 42*(4), 402–420.

Baker, H. J, & Leland, B. (1959). *Detroit tests of learning aptitude.* Indianapolis, IN: Bobbs-Merrill.

Barrowclough, C., Haddock, G., Lobban, F., Jones, S., Siddle, R., Roberts, C., & Gregg, L. (2006). Group cognitive-behavioural therapy for schizophrenia. *The British Journal of Psychiatry, 189*(6), 527–532.

Bechdolf, A., Knost, B., Nelson, B., Schneider, N., Veith, V., Yung, A., & Pukrop, R. (2010). Randomized comparison of group cognitive behaviour therapy and group psychoeducation in acute patients with schizophrenia: Effects on subjective quality of life. *Australian and New Zealand Journal of Psychiatry, 44*(2), 144–150.

Beck, A., Baruch, E., Balter, J. M., Steer, R. A., & Warman, D. M. (2004). A new instrument for measuring insight: The Beck Cognitive Insight Scale. *Schizophrenia Research, 68*(2), 319–329.

Beck, A., Rector, N., Stolar, N., & Grant, P. (2009). *Schizophrenia. Cognitive theory, research and therapy.* New York: Guilford Press.

Beck, A., Steer, R. A., & Brown, G. K. (1996). *Beck depression inventory.* San Antonio, TX: The psychological corporation.

Birchwood, M., Smith, J. O., Cochrane, R., Wetton, S., & Copestake, S. O. N. J. A. (1990). The Social Functioning Scale. The development and validation of a new scale of social adjustment for use in family intervention programmes with schizophrenic patients. *The British Journal of Psychiatry, 157*(6), 853–859.

Butler, L., Johns, L. C., Byrne, M., Joseph, C., O. D. E., Jolley, S., ... Oliver, J. E. (2016). In practice: Running acceptance and commitment for psychosis in community settings. *Journal of Contextual Behavioral Science, 5*(1), 33–38.

Chadwick, P., & Birchwood, M. (1995). The omnipotence of voices. II: The Beliefs About Voices Questionnaire (BAVQ). *The British Journal of Psychiatry, 166*(6), 773–776.

Chadwick, P., Lees, S., & Birchwood, M. A. X. (2000). The revised Beliefs About Voices Questionnaire (BAVQ-R). *The British Journal of Psychiatry, 177*(3), 229–232.

Chadwick, P., Sambrooke, S., Rasch, S., & Davies, E. (2000). Challenging the omnipotence of voices: Group cognitive behavior therapy for voices. *Behaviour Research and Therapy, 38*(10), 993–1003.

Dillon, J., & Hornstein, G. A. (2013). Hearing voices peer support groups: A powerful alternative for people in distress. *Psychosis, 5*(3), 286–295.

Haddock, G., McCarron, J., Tarrier, N., & Faragher, E. B. (1999). Scales to measure dimensions of hallucinations and delusions: The psychotic symptom rating scales (PSYRATS). *Psychological medicine, 29*(4), 879–889.

Harris, R. (2009). ACT made simple: An easy to read primer on Acceptance and Commitment Therapy. Oakland, CA: New Harbinger.

Hayes, S.C., Strosahl, K. D., Wilson, K. G. (1999). *Acceptance and commitment therapy: An experiential approach to behavior change.* New York: Guilford Press.

Hazell, C. M., Greenwood, K., Fielding-Smith, S., Rammou, A., Bogen-Johnston, L., Berry, C., & ... Hayward, M. (2018). Understanding the barriers to accessing symptom-specific cognitive behavior therapy (CBT) for distressing voices: Reflecting on and extending the lessons learnt from the CBT for psychosis literature. *Frontiers in Psychology, 9.*

Hendry, G. L. (2011). *What are the experiences of those attending a self-help hearing voices group: An interpretive phenomenological approach.* University of Leeds.

Hustig, H. H., & Hafner, R. J. (1990). Persistent auditory hallucinations and their relationship to delusions and mood. *The Journal of Nervous and Mental Disease, 178*(4), 264–267.

Johns, L., Oliver, J., Khondoker, M., Byrne, M., Jolley, S., Wykes, C., Joseph, C., Butler, L., Craig, T., & Morris, E. (2015). The feasibility and acceptability of a brief Acceptance and Commitment Therapy (ACT) group intervention for people with psychosis: The 'ACT for Life" study. *Journal of Behavior Therapy and Experimental Psychiatry, 50,* 257–263.

Jones, N., Marino, C., & Hansen, M. (2015). The Hearing Voices Movement in United States: Findings from a national survey of group. *Psychosis, 8*(2), 106–117.

Kay, S. R., Fiszbein, A., & Opfer, L. A. (1987). The positive and negative syndrome scale (PANSS) for schizophrenia. *Schizophrenia Bulletin, 13*(2), 261.

Kelly, G. A. (1955). *The Psychology of Personal Constructs, vols. 1 and 2.* New York: Norton (reprinted by Routledge, 1991).

Kingdon, D. G., & Turkington, D. (2005). *Guides to individualized evidence-based treatment. Cognitive therapy of schizophrenia.* New York: Guilford Press.

Kuipers, E., Yesufu-Udechuku, A., Taylor, C., & Kendall, T. (2014). Management of psychosis and schizophrenia in adults: summary of updated NICE guidance. *BMJ: British Medical Journal, 348*(7945), 33–35.

Leach, M. J. (2005). Rapport: A key to treatment success. *Complementary Therapies in Clinical Practice, 11*(4), 262–265.

Lecomte, T., Leclerc, C., Wykes, T. (2012). Group CBT for early psychosis—are there still benefits one year later? *International Journal of Group Psychotherapy*, 62(2), 309–321.

Lee, K., Hannan, C., Van Den Bosch, J., Williams, J., & Mouratoglou, V. (2002). Evaluating a hearing voices group for older people: Preliminary findings. *International Journal of Geriatric Psychiatry, 17*(11), 1079–1080.

Lincoln, T. M., & Peters, E. (2018). A systematic review and discussion of symptom specific cognitive behavioural approaches to delusions and hallucinations. *Schizophrenia Research.* https://doi-org.proxy.myunion.edu/10.1016/j.schres.2017.12.014.

Louise, S. Fitzpatrick, M., Strauss, C., Rossell, S. L., & Thomas, N. (2018). Mindfulness and acceptance-based interventions for psychosis: Our current understanding and a meta-analysis. *Schizophrenia Research, 192*, 57–63.

Meddings, S., Walley, L., Collings, T., Tullett, F., McEwan, B., & Owen, K. (2004). Are hearing voices groups effective? A preliminary evaluation. *Journal of Psychiatric & Mental Health Nursing, 7*, 135–141.

Morris, E. M. J., Johns, L. C., & Oliver, J. E. (Eds.). (2013). *Acceptance and commitment therapy and mindfulness for psychosis.* Malden, MA: Wiley-Blackwell.

Morrison, A. P., Renton, J. C., Dunn, H., Williams, S., & Bentall, R. P. (2004). *Cognitive Therapy for Psychosis. A formulation-based approach.* New York: Brunner-Routledge.

Ozerengin, M. F., & Cowen, M. A. (1974). Environmental noise level is a factor in the treatment of hospitalized schizophrenics. *Diseases of the nervous system, 35*(5), 241–243.

Paley, G., & Lawton, D. (2001). Evidence-based practice: Accounting for the importance of the therapeutic relationship in UK National Health Service therapy provision. *Counselling and Psychotherapy Research, 1*(1), 12–17.

Penn, D. L., Meyer, P. S., Evans, E., Wirth, R. J., Cai, K., & Burchinal, M. (2009). A randomized controlled trial of group cognitive-behavioral therapy vs. enhanced supportive therapy for auditory hallucinations. *Schizophrenia Research, 109*(1–3), 52–59.

Peters, E., Landau, S., McCrone, P., Cooke, M., Fisher, P., Steel, C., Evans, R., Carswell, K., Dawson, K., Williams, S., Howard, A., & Kuiper, E. (2010). A randomised controlled trial of cognitive behaviour therapy for psychosis in a routine clinical service. *Acta Psychiatr Scand, 122*(4), 302–318.

Rosenberg, M. (1965). *Society and the adolescent self-image.* Princeton, NJ: Princeton University Press.

Ruddle, A., Mason, O., & Wykes, T. (2011). A review of hearing voices groups: Evidence and mechanisms of change. *Clinical Psychology Review, 31*(5), 757–766.

Sciarappa, K., Rogers, E. S., & Chamberlin, J. (1994). A consumer constructed empowerment scale to measure empowerment among users of mental health services. *Psychiatric Services, 48*(8), 1042–1047.

Shawyer, F., Farhall, J., Thomas, N., Hayes, S. C., Gallop, R., Copolov, D., & Castle, D. J. (2017). Acceptance and commitment therapy for psychosis: Randomised controlled trial. *British Journal of Psychiatry, 210*(2), 140–148.

Thomas, N., Hayward, M., Peters, E., van der Gaag, M., Bentall, R. P., Jenner, J., Strauss, C., Sommer, I. E., Johns, L. C., Varese, F., García-Montes, J. M., Waters, F., Dodgson, G., & … McCarthy-Jones, S. (2014). Psychological therapies for auditory hallucinations (voices): current status and key directions for future research. *Schizophrenia bulletin, 40*(Suppl. 4), S202–12.

Webb, J. (2011). *Hearing voices: coping, resilience and recovery.* University of Leeds.

Wykes, T., Parr, A., & Landau, S. (1999). Group treatment of auditory hallucinations: Exploratory study of effectiveness. *British Journal of Psychiatry, 175*, 180–185.

Wykes, T., Steel, C., Everitt, B., & Tarrier, N. (2008). Cognitive behavior therapy for schizophrenia: Effect sizes, clinical models, and methodological rigor. *Schizophrenia Bulletin, 34*(3), 523–537.

Yalom, I., & Leszcz, M. (2005). *The theory and practice of group psychotherapy* (5th ed.). New York, NY: Basic Books.

Zigmond, A. S., & Snaith, R. P. (1983). The hospital anxiety and depression scale. *Acta Psychiatrica Scandinavica, 67*(6), 361–370.

4

IMPORTANCE OF ENSURING EMOTIONAL SAFETY

Creating a Safe Atmosphere for All

> *Reflection: In what context do you feel safe in disclosing your most personal thoughts and feelings to others? How can you cultivate this awareness to help create an atmosphere within your groups or therapy environments to help others feel secure enough to discuss sensitive material?*

All the facilitators with whom I spoke discussed the importance of creating physical and/or emotional safety within their hearing voices groups. While creating a holding space of safety may seem to be an obvious goal for any group, cultivating a safe space for folks who hear voices, have visions, or experience unusual beliefs is crucial. When I first sought treatment for my voice hearing experiences (both in the hospital and subsequently with an outpatient therapist), I was confused, ashamed, and could not trust my perceptions of the world around me. Places like my home and my car, which previously felt like safe havens, felt unsafe. At one point, I believed someone had planted a bomb under my car and asked a friend to drive me home after a dinner out. (I was too embarrassed to admit my *real* reasons for asking for the ride and instead lied, "I'm having car trouble.") When I was hospitalized, I felt somewhat more "contained," and grateful for the sense of containment. I did not feel the staff or other clients would hurt me, but the voices continued to cause problems. Even within a contained locked psychiatric unit, I felt unsafe. Therefore, hearing group facilitators talk about the necessity for emotional safety really resonated with me.

How does one provide safety to a group of folks who often cannot trust their own senses, perceptions, and thoughts? Based on lived experience and work as a facilitator, I discovered normalizing the experiences and explaining why these voices/visions may be occurring can be very useful. Neither my inpatient therapists nor the outpatient therapists I subsequently saw provided any normalization or psychoeducation regarding my experiences. Had such information been provided, I would have felt like FINALLY! someone had thrown me a life preserver, because I was drifting in shame and confusion. I would have felt safe.

Subtypes of Voices and Neuroscience

While no single explanation can account for the phenomenological diversity of peoples' voice hearing experiences, nearly all the individuals who attend my voices group have reported trauma histories, and trauma was a significant trigger for my own voice hearing experiences (Bless et al., 2018; McCarthy-Jones & Resnick, 2014; Jones, 2010). McCarthy-Jones et al. (2014) proposed five distinct subtypes of voices to help clients, researchers, and clinicians make sense of and respond to these experiences in a helpful manner: Hypervigilance, Autobiographical Memory, Inner Speech, Epileptic, and Deafferentation.

These proposed subtypes provide psychological and physiological phenomenological explanations, and do not account for the spiritual reasons that people may have voices/visions. Clients who believe themselves possessed by demons or evil spirits often fall into two categories: those who believe only a priest/preacher can help remove these entities and clients, and those who are open to using talk therapy and medications. I have also worked with clients who perceive their voices and visions as spiritual experiences (e.g., spirit guides, angels, God, demon possession) and/or identify as psychics, prophets, or mediums. I will discuss how I typically work with these folks to promote client validation, group cohesiveness, and above all, SAFETY (makes sense—as this is what this chapter is all about).

Hypervigilant Auditory Type

The hypervigilance subtype of voice hearing is supported by the research efforts of Dodgson and Gordon (2009) and Garwood, Dodgson, Bruce, and McCarthy-Jones (2015), which suggest stressful life events or drug use trigger an emotionally upsetting "high-alert" state in a person. The person becomes hypervigilant for threatening sounds, people, objects, etc., decreasing their ability to detect threats in their environment, and increasing the chance of auditory "false-positives" (such as hearing noises confirming anxiety fueled-beliefs or safety-related fears of persecution). How can this occur? Well, generally speaking, humans prefer to avoid danger and stay healthy, happy, and whole. Humans have developed attentional biases towards threats of danger as a way of staying alive. How does this relate to hypervigilant voices?

A lot of research models exist about attentional biases, and all cite *facilitated attention* as a key component (Cisler & Koster, 2010). What does that even mean? Imagine an individual who has been exposed to abuse or repeated stressful situations. Perhaps this person had inadequate coping skills and discovered illegal drugs to help numb the anxiety but had to navigate the stressful daily task of obtaining illegal drugs (Who can you trust? Is my dealer a police informant? Is someone going to steal my drugs while I sleep?). Anxiety within the individual increases, and he/she may quickly become attentive to any noise, creak, or whisper which suggests danger or someone about to snatch their drugs. This phenomenon, *facilitated attention,* is the speed at which one's attention is drawn to a threatening noise, person, obnoxious smell, etc. People experiencing hypervigilant type (HV) report hearing either a voice or sounds (e.g., laughter, their name being called, derogatory slurs) with threatening content, which is perceived as coming from the external environment (Garwood, Dodgson, Bruce, & McCarthy-Jones, 2015). Hypervigilant voice hearers want to remain safe, so their attention is quickly drawn to suspicious noises, and per some of the attentional bias models, folks have a difficult time shifting their attention away from the threatening voices (Cisler & Koster, 2010).

Autobiographical Voices Type

Autobiographical voices are connected to either traumatic events or frequent adversity (e.g., a caregiver who frequently made demeaning remarks, childhood bullies, or an angry spouse) in which messages were repeated multiple times (McCarthy-Jones et al., 2014). Voices which fall under this category may be verbatim repetitions of what was said at the time of the trauma or adverse events, or may not accurately reflect what was said. This subtype can be further broken down into subcategories: dissociative and non-dissociative. A risk related to PTSD involves decreased hippocampal processing of the traumatic event, so the related memories are not properly time-stamped and integrated into long-term memory in an organized way. This could lead to splintered trauma-related memories with sensory properties reaching the conscious mind with little to no context. Scary and confusing, right? McCarthy-Jones et al. (2014) proposed that these types of voices could be conceptualized as occurring due to a faulty connection between the amygdala and hippocampus, which often occurs for trauma sufferers. Non-dissociative voices are memories of speech, but due to a glitch in context, the memories are experienced as voices occurring in the present. Many of my group clients experience autobiographical voices, so this is a concept we often discuss within the group in great detail.

Inner Speech Type

The third subcategory is *inner speech*, which is broken down further into three experiences: obsessional, novel, and own thought (McCarthy-Jones et al., 2014). Obsessional refers to brief and repetitive voices that compel one to act and often are perceived as commands. These may be related to the obsessional thoughts common to Obsessive Compulsive Disorder. No neurobiological work has yet been researched with this subtype. I am familiar with this subtype, as I have a long-term client who lives with these types of voices. Margot, a female client of mine in her mid-60s, was diagnosed with schizoaffective disorder when she was in her mid-20s. She routinely hears voices throughout her day.

At my behest, she began keeping a journal of her voices, and after several years of monitoring them, she noticed they typically consist of one-word or (at most) two-word phrases. She tells me the words do not vary much beyond "chirp," "soon," or "ugh." These words have little to no meaning for Margot, and do not seem to be attached to any particular memories or other external triggers.

Novel voices (e.g., running commentaries) may also be rooted in *inner speech*, and commands may occur. However, the commands (unlike the obsessional voices) are longer in duration. Novel voices may be related to the failure of corollary-discharge, in which the hearer has difficulty distinguishing externally generated perceptions from internally generated perceptions (Ford & Mathalon, 2005).

Finally, own thought voices is where an individual confuses inner monologue with voices (McCarthy-Jones et al., 2014). Again, there is not much neurological support for this subtype to date, but I have worked with a number of clients who struggle with differentiating between their inner monologue and their perceptions of voices.

Case Example: Adele

Adele is an African American woman in her mid-50s with a diagnosis of schizoaffective disorder and a history of neglect and abuse. When Adele becomes stressed, sad, or overwhelmed, she will check herself into my clinic's voluntary crisis unit. She often reports difficulties distinguishing between "what I'm thinking versus the voices I am hearing." Adele said this problem becomes more exaggerated when she feels severe levels of depression or anxiety. After speaking with Adele about her predicament (how does one confuse internal dialogue with voices?), she explained, "The voices say things which I don't agree with and don't go along with the way I think. They may say, 'That man is ugly! Look how ugly he is!' But I—the Adele part of my mind—doesn't agree. I would never think that about that guy, because he's my friend, but the voices say it over and over. I can't get them out of my mind, and then I begin to wonder if I do feel that way. It's very confusing." Adele's voices appear to be ego dystonic and repetitive, yet her poor sense of core self makes distinguishing the inner monologue from voices a challenge.

Epileptic Voices Type

Subtype four are *epileptic* voices, and based upon phenomenology and neurology, these form a discrete, separate category which can only be identified through an epilepsy diagnosis. Psychoses of epilepsy are generally classified into three main patterns: *ictal, postictal,* and *interictal* (Sachdev, 1998). Ictal psychosis occurs concurrently with epileptic seizures, and hallucinations or delusions are not present. Instead, a person may present with disorganized thoughts and behaviors, but insight remains intact. Postictal psychosis (PIP) occurs when a seizure is followed by psychosis-related symptoms. PIP typically begins with anxiety, insomnia, and feelings of oppression before symptoms such as voices, visions, unusual beliefs, catatonia, mania, or depressive moods occur (Falip, Carreno, Donaire et al., 2009; Irwin, & Fortune, 2014). Interictal psychosis (IIP) does not occur around the onset of a seizure and can even occur when seizures are infrequent (Sachdev, 1998). IIP episodes last for several days or weeks, present with mood symptoms, paranoid ideation, auditory hallucinations, and "mystical experiences" (Irwin, & Fortune, 2014). Although diagnosing and treating epilepsy-related psychosis is beyond the scope of mental health practitioners, we should be aware of possible medical causes of voices/visions if intending to work with this population.

Deafferentation-Related Voices Type

The last subcategory is *deafferentation*-related voices, which present as continuous. Their content is frequently musical, but not always. Neurologically, they are conceptualized as resulting from a deafferentation (an incomplete connection) from the auditory cortex and other language perception areas. These types of AVH may be elicited by social isolation or hearing problems (McCarthy-Jones et al., 2014).

Spiritual Voices/Mystical Voices

Researchers, who discuss different types of voices, do not discuss spiritually based voices and visions, but many of the clients who attend my groups believe their voices/visions/unusual tactile experiences are religious or spiritual in nature. In the words of Annie Lennox, "Who am I to disagree?" I have worked with clients from all types of spiritual backgrounds, including pagan priests/priestesses, exorcists, prophets, mediums, psychics, and those who believe in animal totems, spirit guides, angels, and demons. One of my regular clients often said she came to group because "I'm a prophet in my church, but the other church members get uncomfortable when I talk about this. So I come here and tell you all! I can't help it if I have a message to share with someone, and I usually do—I'll pull them aside after church." Group members often use sessions to discuss psychic abilities, spirit guides, angels, and the efficacy of non-Western interventions such as crystals, sage, and palo santo. One group member, who identified as "psychic," shared her frustrations about being followed by "the ghost of my boyfriend's dead girlfriend. I want her to leave me alone." (This client found that carrying a particular crystal, which she dubbed her "ghost crystal," kept the spirit of the dead girlfriend away.)

Using non-Western medicine-related tools like crystals, sage, and pendulums is beyond the scope of my knowledge, but I recognize how helpful my clients find these tools. When someone expresses interest in non-Western tools or spiritual guidance, I (thankfully) have a list of resources—depending upon the need—which I refer them to seek out. I would encourage anyone who is planning to run a voices group to develop a resource list of their own, and to be judicious in the referrals. I personally check out each person, book, website, and article prior to making my referrals, because I would never want a client to be harmed, misled, or taken advantage of financially. Additionally, when clients indicate they are having what they suspect to be a spiritual issue (e.g., a haunting or a demon possession), I offer up an appropriate resource, but also encourage them to consider that the issue at hand may be more down-to-earth (heh-heh) in nature. This occurred recently in group when a client stated he was having sleep difficulties. He found himself moving a lot in his bed at night, and said, "I think I might be possessed by a demon." After offering the client the name of a local clergywoman knowledgeable in such matters, I gently suggested his sleep issues could also be related to a psychiatric or medical issue—or both. The client thought about my feedback and said, "You know, you could be right! I'll talk with my doctor and psychiatrist too."

Finally, a word of caution about clients who report demon possession, hauntings, or other fear-inducing spiritual experiences: Safety first! If the client's functioning is rapidly deteriorating, and they appear to be an active (e.g., homicidal or suicidal) or passive (e.g., not bathing, unable to complete activities of daily living) danger to self or others, hospitalization may be necessary to get the client stabilized *BEFORE* calling in the exorcist, shaman, or local psychic medium.

Hypnagogic- and Hypnopompic-Related Voices (and Visions)

When I was first working in the mental health field, I had an 8-year-old client, Jamie, who told me about the "scary things" he saw when first waking up in the morning. Jamie indicated he saw "couches with spikes" moving towards him in the morning. Working as a community-based therapist at the time, I saw inside his house and specifically his bedroom, and there were no spike-studded couches in the area (or anything remotely resembling such an object). I consulted with my clinical supervisor and the agency's psychiatrist, who both agreed Jamie's vision was likely a hypnopompic hallucination. For those unfamiliar with hypnopompic and hypnagogic hallucinations, as they are clinically termed, they occur when one is falling asleep (hypnagogic hallucinations) and/or waking up (hypnopompic hallucinations). These experiences are fairly common (found in up to 70% of the general population), with visual phenomena (e.g., hypnagogia), usually made up of shapes, light flashes, and images of animals or people, being less common (Waters et al., 2016). Voices and other sounds (e.g., music, phones ringing, doors slamming, people talking) are less common. Somatic or bodily experiences like falling, sensing a presence in the room, flying, or feelings of weightlessness can also occur. Hypnopompic experiences usually are continuations of dreams when one is first waking up (Waters et al., 2016). Researchers believe hypnagogic experiences are also the extension of a dream/sleep state (e.g., part of sleep state one that terminate by sleep state two) (Speth, Venzel, & Voss, 2013).

Alcohol- and Drug-Related Voices

A lot of times I meet folks whose voices started while using or withdrawing from drugs and/or alcohol. The Diagnostic and Statistical Manual of Mental Disorders (5th ed.; DSM-5; American Psychiatric Association, 2013) indicates "hallucinations" are symptoms of alcohol withdrawal, cannabis intoxication, hallucinogen intoxication, phencyclidine (e.g., PCP) intoxication, opioid intoxication, sedative withdrawal, and stimulant intoxication. These types of extreme state experiences typically last the length of the detox, but the duration depends upon how long the individual was using the particular substance. I once spoke with a client who was experiencing voices several weeks after detoxing from alcohol, but she had been abusing alcohol for 30-plus years. Additionally, voices/visions can occur due to Hallucinogen Persisting Perception Disorder, which can last weeks, months, and in some cases, years after drug use (American Psychiatric Association, 2013). Typically (in my experience), folks with these issues do not show up to my groups. However, I did have one female client who attended my Voices and Visions group for a year to better understand the frightening visions she experienced while detoxing from alcohol years before. She reported only seeing visions during a discrete period of time during her detox, but the experience spooked her nonetheless.

I wanted to outline the different types of voices people can experience and their possible causes to illustrate how confusing, intrusive, scary, and socially isolating these experiences can be for folks. Many of their extreme state experiences are closely reminiscent of previous unsafe and terrifying environments in which they previously lived. Therefore, creating a safe and welcoming environment is crucial to having a successful group.

Creating Safety

In order for emotional safety to be created, most of the expert facilitators I interviewed mentioned noticing that group clients were more willing to share with one another when the group room felt physically safe and containing. One of the facilitators with whom I spoke explained the importance of creating a physically safe space for this client population:

> *I think the patients do need to be comfortable to look at really disturbing and intimidating experiences so … you need to think about the setting to be as containing and holding as possible because they feel so persecuted inside so maybe having [a] sterile or formal environment in the group would be difficult.*

The Group Room

Several facilitators stated the configuration of the group room (e.g., the room size, if there was a table in the room, whether the clients could clearly see exits and doors) impacts how willingly the clients will share in group:

> *If you have got a bunch of paranoid folks, you have got to have less guys or bigger rooms, so there's enough room and they are not trapped.*
>
> *I have found that it's really important to have a room where there are windows and people can see the exit. I am working with folks that have a lot of trauma history, who have been contained against their will. So sometimes we have to use another room when*

> *the "good room" is taken up, and the group does not go as well. [Although] we do have a window to the outside, people can't see the exit and the elevators. People get to feeling a little cornered … [and] the group does not go as well.*

In the room where I facilitate my group, the door leading in and out of the room causes many clients to feel frustrated and anxious. The doorknob does not twist easily, and the heavy door requires the dexterity of an NBA player to efficiently yank it open. (Fast footwork, quick hand-eye coordination, sweating, and upper body strength are required.) One of my group participants, Rachel, who is very petite, hates the door so much that she refuses to sit in the room until everyone has entered. Once, she accidentally was the last group member to leave, and because of her petite status, was unable to hoist the door open on her own. Rachel later told me, "I thought no one would rescue me! I couldn't get out!" Eventually staff entered the room and freed her, but this client's anxiety had morphed into terror! Our group's solution for this dilemma (because naturally, the door cannot remain open during group) was to place duct tape over the door catch. The tape is peeled off after each group (otherwise there would be fire code hazards or some such), and the door is re-taped by me prior to group. Consequently, clients can more easily yank the door open if they need to escape quickly or (as with Rachel) are unable to open the door on their own.

Clients in my groups also have particular chairs they like sitting in during group. Facilitators with whom I spoke also indicated this was common for their groups. Over the years, clients have explained to me that they like to either see the door or to have certain walls at their backs for protection. One long-term client once explained why having his eyes to the group room door was crucial. "I grew up in a bar, which my parents owned. I liked to keep my eyes on the door even then to know who or what was about to jump off at any time. If I saw trouble coming, I knew to run for it or hide under a table."

Screening Group Members

Several expert facilitators said they screen out potential group members who are severely distressed (e.g., physically aggressive towards others, speaking in a severely disorganized manner) because these clients would be disruptive and could cause other clients to feel unsafe, frustrated, or shut down. Below are their comments on the importance of screening:

> *Head banging constantly … things like that. Those folks never made it to group because those who were grossly impaired because of their thought processes like word salad, neologisms, and concept disorganization things like that. We would rule those people out because they were almost non-verbal.*
>
> *I would attempt not to include participants before they have partially calmed down … unless a patient was unrestrainable, everybody was invited.*

When I run groups in our clinic's crisis unit, I encounter folks who are really struggling with managing their psychosis-related symptoms. Attempting to conduct group with clients who present with disorganized speech/thoughts, exceptionally disruptive behaviors (such as unexpectedly moving around the room in an unpredictable and ostentatious manner), or who spend the entire group solely engaged with their voices/visions (mumbling and laughing to clearly internalized stimuli) can be disruptive and frustrating to other group members. Therefore, I also screen who attends my voices group. I do not permit clients into the group who are aggressive, extremely disruptive (e.g., shouting, unable to sit in a room for an hour, engaging in excessive disruptive movement), who display little interest in discussing their experiences with others, or are cognitively disorganized and/or verbally hostile towards others.

Over the years, I have worked with folks in my voices groups who have a wide variety of personality types, socioeconomic backgrounds, and levels of functioning. Through all these experiences, clients in my Voices and Visions groups are generally friendly, creative, wise, funny, empathic, and eager to connect with others who, as my one client said recently, "have experiences like mine!" My interactions with my Voices and Visions group members remind me why I love working in the field of mental health.

Executive Dysfunction

One of the facilitators I interviewed stressed the importance of learning about a client's "context" (e.g., histories of substance abuse, traumatic brain injuries, and physical/emotional/sexual abuse) prior to allowing them a spot in the group:

> *You could be setting yourself up (or both of you) for a crisis, because if somebody has significant brain damage [caused by trauma, substance abuse, or brain injuries], even though it may not be readily apparent, [the client] may not be able to physiologically manage the impulses that get stirred up by more in-depth work … That way you just know if they have those issues, you just have to go slower, and before you get too in-depth in any particular piece, be very mindful of how they are reacting to it.*

I too prefer to be very clear about clients' context prior to them joining the group. Learning if a potential group member has significant executive functioning deficits helps me in the group screening process. I will ask the referring clinician, nurse, or doctor if the client has major problems in the following areas: impulse control, emotional control, planning/organization, working memory, processing speed, shift, perseverance, self-awareness/monitoring, and task monitoring. All of us (including group facilitators) struggle with these domains when stressed or upset, and I wouldn't necessarily prevent a client from attending if they struggled with ALL domains. However, I want to know what I am working with if the person is new to me.

Case Example: Haley

Haley is a 20-something female with schizoaffective disorder, a history of multiple concussions, and a long history of physical abuse. She regularly attended my voices group and also works with me individually. As Haley began to trust me, she became more open about her thoughts towards other women. She is self-conscious about her appearance, and would routinely tell me, "I saw these girls at the gym. Seriously, they were SO pretty, I wanted to stab them in their perfect faces." Haley also reported experiencing command voices telling her to stab these women, but she insisted that she had no intent to act upon the voices. When I first heard about these command voices, I was (needless to say) a bit concerned, assessed her for a criminal history (none to speak of), and frequently consulted about her case with my clinical supervisor. Over time, Haley discovered her animosity towards these women was a mixture of anger at her own body/appearance, jealousy of their looks, her desire to date these women, and fear they may reject her romantically. After working together for several years, Haley learned to manage her voices through cultivating a healthy support system, working with a patient and open-minded prescriber, healthy eating, exercise (away from gyms, which were a trigger), and talking to her therapist (me).

Sure, there were times I would insist Haley admit herself to the clinic's crisis unit when symptoms were severe. However, my awareness of her context, our shared (dark) sense of humor, and our rapport cultivated a solid therapeutic relationship. When I noticed Haley's symptoms worsening and told her, "It's unit time," she would declare me to be a "pain in [her] ass," but she would admit herself to the crisis unit immediately. Had I been unaware of her context (e.g., history of head trauma, abuse history, schizoaffective disorder, drug abuse history), I might not have responded to Haley's symptoms effectively, and our rapport would not have been as good.

Validation

Many of the facilitators I interviewed mentioned that they cultivate an environment of emotional safety for the clients through validation of their experiences and by treating them with respect.

Why might validation be so essential for this particular client population? A few of the facilitators stated that the clients who attend these groups often feel "misunderstood," "marginalized," and/or "dismissed" by their loved ones, people in their communities, and mental health professionals:

> *People might say, "You need to take a pill" or "You know, that's really bizarre and I can't hang out with you anymore." Or if people do really understand it and it connects to trauma and they're part of the family, they may not be able to hear it ... Folks already come in being shut down and misunderstood, so the most important thing to do is hang out with them about it.*
>
> *I wonder how many times (these) clients hear "you're crazy" or something like that? So to just be able to mention it to somebody and not say you're crazy is helpful.*

Several of the facilitators mentioned clients who have voices/visions are frequently taken advantage of by others because of their perceptual difficulties, and nearly all the facilitators stated that many voice hearers isolate from others because they feel misunderstood. I have learned that isolation can take on different forms—they may be social butterflies with regards to their friends or family but clam up when talking about their extreme state experiences. On the other hand, clients who have these experiences may socially withdraw from others altogether. The desire or ability to connect with others differs from person to person. Group therapy, according to nearly all the facilitators, can decrease the desire to isolate because clients are in contact with others who are validating their experiences.

> *To meet someone who is like you in some way. People feel so alien ... It's huge not to be isolated! You can't really get out of your isolation if you can't talk about what your life is like. And I think people can talk uniquely with somebody who is similar to [them]. I can really communicate most freely with somebody who is like me.*

Another way in which several of the facilitators encourage the feeling of validation is to address relevant issues which arise during the group discussion (e.g., concerns about inattentive nurses and doctors, frustrations with medications, the departure or death of a group member). When asked why addressing relevant issues with this particular client population is important, one group facilitator replied:

> *Because the relevant stuff is in the present ... It's really happening to them and it's affecting them. One of the things that has happened quite frequently to individuals with perceptual disturbances is invalidation and devaluation ... so if there are things that are troublesome, these folks have learned over time not to talk about it because there is no point in talking about it. [Therefore], to provide them with a more corrective emotional experience, to be able to bring that out of them, and take the role of someone who wants to validate them and care about their lived experience. That can promote the continuity of their experiential presence with themselves but also the attachment they receive to other individuals.*

Nearly half of the group facilitators that I interviewed stated that encouraging their clients to share their experiences and feel validated also results in clients developing increased solid support systems both in the group (e.g., developing friendships with other group members) or within the community (e.g., their town, the hospital, or the prison). I know things are going well for group members when I hear about them seeking out friends or family with whom they can spend time. Sometimes group members socialize with one another (although I strongly discourage romantic relationships between group members—way too messy) and develop lasting friendships.

Respect My Authority—Regarding My Voices!

Treating clients with respect and encouraging them to treat one another with respect is another factor many of the expert facilitators frequently mentioned as important for good group outcomes. One way to foster respect, according to several facilitators, is to look for the similarities between ourselves and the clients and not view the clients with condescension. As one facilitator explained:

> *I think treating clients as human beings, who experience the exact same experience as the therapist, is helpful … And what's not helpful is the idea that there is a big difference between the therapist and the patient in the sense the therapist considers himself "sane" and, um, "healthy" … What's much more helpful is to look at the similarities between the patient and the therapist.*

Group leaders with whom I spoke explained that treating clients in this fashion prevents them from feeling "dehumanized" or "alien," which is a common occurrence within this client population. One of my personal biggest pet peeves are therapists and other mental health providers who treat clients with false flattery, phony displays of interest, and/or in a paternalistic manner. Having been a client, I know when the therapist is putting on a false display of friendliness or a sickly-sweet show of "concern." My group clients have told me when *they* suspect certain therapists are fakes. Just because a client presents with symptoms which occasionally impact their sense of reality does *NOT* mean they are not paying attention to your behavior and attitude as a therapist.

In my experience, many clients who have voices and visions seem to have a heightened sensitivity for judgmental clinicians who lack sincerity. Conducting a voices and visions group is not akin to running a human petting zoo. You are not there to marvel at their "otherness," pity them, or view them as incapable of much growth or change. Clients do not attend group looking to be infantilized, thank you very much.

Some of the wisest observations about life have come from comments made by group members. When I come into the group room, I'm just as flawed, weird, and human as anyone else there. Sure, I recognize the power differential, but I work hard through my words, presentation, and body language to join the conversation, be part of the dialogue, and not simply *lead it.* Creating this culture of acceptance is an important part in helping folks to feel safe.

Respect Differences

Several of the expert facilitators stated that another way to foster respect is to encourage clients to be respectful of one another's differences (e.g., views on the etiology of psychosis, cultural beliefs, views on spirituality and psychosis-related symptoms). One of the facilitators stated that when one or several members are rigid in their views on the etiology of psychosis-related symptoms, it can cause the other group members to shut down:

> *I think one of the things that get in the way is that people who have these experiences have been through a lot of medicalizing and pathologizing of their experience … getting people to look at their voices in a different way I think is hard … I'm not saying no one should feel that way ever. But if … they don't get curious … I think it's one of the things that makes the groups hard … I think a lot of people consider themselves as having either spiritual experiences, or there's [sic] these entities that they talk to.*

Two facilitators also mentioned how monitoring and adjusting the language they use with clients fosters an environment of respect within the group.

One facilitator stated that he monitors how much empathy he uses with clients to avoid invading his clients' emotional boundaries too quickly:

> *People are psychotic because they can't deal with what is going on inside them, so if you take somebody, who by definition cannot deal with what is going on inside of them and you get overly empathetic, you are going to drive them nuts! Sometimes the thing to say is rather than "you seem really angry about that" is "now that really sucks!" … because "hurts" is way too close to home …*

> *They are not there yet ... that can get refined when they are ready to hear "that hurts" and feel "that hurts."*

I find myself being very judicious in the type of language I use with clients, particularly in my voices group. Group members have repeatedly told me they take offense when a therapist "comes in too hot" with a line of questioning—particularly if that therapist does not have a good rapport with the client.

Most of the facilitators did not utilize terms like delusions and hallucinations when discussing their clients' psychosis-related experiences. One facilitator stated she purposely uses non-pathologizing language when discussing the clients' experiences during the group, because utilizing pathologizing language (e.g., hallucinations, delusions) can lead to the dehumanization and marginalization of clients with psychosis-related symptoms:

> *Part of it has to do with getting away from some of the pathologizing language ... trying to get away from some of the language that has unfortunately resulted in or has been part of dehumanizing people and marginalizing them and voices and visions ... if someone comes along and says well it's just a hallucination, and it's not real ... people have very marked, emotional reactions to that and that doesn't help anything.*

Harmful Voices

Often in my groups, folks will say they are experiencing voices that command them to kill/harm themselves or others. I always take these comments seriously when they arise but try to remain calm and matter of fact as I inquire about these experiences. Recently, a new client, a 35-year-old female, Serena, showed up in group and stated she has command voices telling her to kill others and providing her with graphic descriptions regarding how she should kill. I asked questions about the intensity of these experiences, her own criminal record, had she physically assaulted anyone in her life, history of head trauma (to assess for impulsivity issues), and how long these voices have been present.

The new client explained, "I have never acted on these voices, have never been in a fight or been arrested. I don't have plans to act out these commands. They just happen, and the urge to act on them is like a 1 (on a scale of 1–10, with 10 being 'severe')." In this case, the situation was fairly simple, with no need to file a mental hygiene warrant on her (maybe called a pink slip in other states?) or invite her to spend time on the community mental health agency's crisis unit. Here are the following questions I ask when someone shares about suicidal or homicidal voices/visions:

- How long have these experiences been happening?
- Have they intensified lately? On a scale of 1–10 (10 = severe), where would you rate your experience currently?
- Do you have any urges to act on these experiences? If so, how would you do it? (I avoid using the word "plan," because I have discovered over the years that folks confuse this term to mean a specific date/time versus a method to act out their homicidal or suicidal voices).
- What will you do/would you do if these experiences intensify?
- Do you have any history of acting on these voices? Have you ever been arrested or hospitalized?
- Have you ever had a concussion, brain injury, or sustained a serious knock to the head?

I prefer getting this type of history when screening people prior to them joining group. However, depending upon the group, your rapport with the client, and your own comfort level, these questions can be asked in the group setting. I have also been known to say to a client, "Hey, I want to check in with you after group and make some suggestions about the intense voices/visions you're experiencing." After group, I can further assess the client and ascertain if they need a higher level of care. Often group members share about experiences they have been experiencing for months or even years. I have several clients whose baseline level of functioning includes having regular homicidal or suicidal voices. I highly recommend reading *The Practical Art of*

Suicide Assessment: A guide for mental health professionals and substance abuse counselors by Dr. Shawn Christopher Shea (2011). As group facilitators, you WILL come up against folks who have command voices to kill themselves or others. Make sure to develop a strong comfort level with risk assessment before conducting a group for voice hearers. Clients with whom I work know I have an even-handed approach to managing risk, and when I tell them "you need to be hospitalized," they rarely argue with me.

(In the interest of full disclosure, I and the other psychologists in my agency are trained in forensic commitment and work with the local court system, namely, county mental hygiene commissioner, to assess who should be detained and if they truly are a danger to themself or others. Therefore, these types of assessments have become second nature to me, but when in doubt—always, ALWAYS consult with other clinicians. I still do.)

Working with Harmful Voices

If a person attends my group and reports homicidal or suicidal voices (or visions) and does not need to be hospitalized, I typically focus on the emotional process of the person's experience. If I sense talking about these experiences makes them uncomfortable, I speak to that and normalize their anxiety: "A lot of folks who come in and talk about the suicidal or homicidal voices find it uncomfortable or it makes them anxious." (Typically there are nods all around from group members). "Who here has had voices that tell them to hurt others or kill themselves? Show of hands?" (There are always a few folks in every crowd. If not, I reassure the person their experience is not uncommon.) "Who here has had voices which say horrible or nasty things to them? When these voices say these mean or rude things to you, what feelings show up? Are you pissed, sad, worried, or maybe some emotion I haven't even mentioned?"

Talking about these experiences helps to decrease people's anxiety about their experiences and models the value of reaching out when rude, nasty, or scary voices show up. If a mean person was saying threatening things to us, we would reach out for support (ideally), so why should talking about voices be different? I do encourage the clients to seek out trusted, safe people who won't freak out when they hear about the person's voices.

Group Facilitator Safety

Every facilitator with whom I spoke also stressed the importance of seeking out supervision and/or support from experienced therapists who have worked with this client population. As one facilitator explained, discussing clients with a supervisor grounds and supports facilitators who work with this client population:

> *The supervisor's, for lack of a better term, advantage, is that he or she is not directly involved in the chaos of the psychosis and has a better view. A further advantage he or she has is that the therapist acts as an endangered but healthy ego that partly filters and organizes that chaos.*

Several facilitators indicated they do not feel supported by many of their mental health colleagues and felt professionally "isolated" because they do fully subscribe to a medical model for the etiology of psychosis-related symptoms or do not believe clients can recover. Therefore, they are grateful for organizations like the Hearing Voices Network or the ISPS. As one of the facilitators stated:

> *[She and her group members] had active hostility and discouragement in [their local] psychiatric community. That's been the biggest problem … Well, um, this problem with opposition, you know from colleagues, is very painful. And being isolated, professionally isolated, is very difficult but it's changing, so that's where ISPS comes in. I mean that's been a lifeline, really a lifeline for me.*

Another facilitator had colleagues who were initially skeptical of the development of a group for this population, or who were "asupportive." Feeling unsupported by colleagues could cause facilitators who run these groups to have a parallel process with their clients:

> *I think we are an anomaly in the mental health field, and … sometimes you're going to get freaked out and be like, "Am I wrong?", because you're having a parallel experience to your clients. Because … everyone is saying, "you're going to make people sicker. You collude with them." I think it's really important for [facilitators, who work with this population] to have their own support networks with people who have the same beliefs as them.*

I am quite lucky to have a couple of supervisors who are familiar with clients, who have voices and visions, and co-workers who support the work I do with my voices and visions group. My supervisors and many of my coworkers know about my history of voice hearing (now the rest get to know when they read this—SURPRISE!). I also have the added bonus of having a supervisor who runs a first episode psychosis program, so he is very familiar with current literature on voice hearing and regularly attends ISPS conferences. Not all group facilitators have such support, and I would encourage the development of more ongoing group training workshops throughout the country.

Summary Points

- Creating physical and emotional safety is particularly important within hearing voices groups in order to run an effective group where members are secure enough to share their most challenging experiences.
- There are five distinct subtypes of voices (as proposed by McCarthy-Jones et al., 2014). These include Hypervigilance, Autobiographical Memory, Inner Speech, Epileptic, and Deafferentation. Reviewing the subtypes can help facilitators better understand and be able to help explain client experiences in a more efficient manner. It's important to recognize that there are different types of voices that people

can experience, which can add to their sense of isolation if not understood.

- Group clients are more willing to share with one another when the group feels physically safe and contained. Facilitators should consider factors such as room size, objects in the room, whether clients can see exits and doors, having windows in rooms, sitting with walls to their backs, etc.
- It is important to screen potential group members to ensure that they can benefit from the group and not compromise the safety of other group members. Individuals who are severely distressed, physically aggressive toward others, speaking in a disorganized fashion, head banging, engaging in unpredictable behaviors, etc. are likely not appropriate for a Hearing Voices group until they are more stable. Client context is also important to consider.
- In order to ensure an atmosphere of emotional safety, it's important to validate the client's experiences and to treat them with respect. Allowing them the opportunity to address relevant issues that arise during the group discussion can go a long way in adding to their sense of feeling validated.
- It's good to keep in mind the similarities between ourselves as facilitators and the clients. Being authentic is important. Clients who experience voices, visions, and unusual thoughts sometimes seem to have a heightened sensitivity for judgmental clinicians lacking sincerity. Foster a culture of genuine acceptance.
- Encourage clients to be respectful of one another's differences as they relate to their cultural beliefs or practices, views on spirituality, symptoms, etc. Developing a good sense of rapport and communicating with an appropriate amount of empathy, and avoiding pathologizing language in discussing client experiences, are important in creating an atmosphere where discussion can be fruitful.
- Group facilitator physical and emotional safety needs must be met as well. Supervision and consultation are particularly important when working with this population.

References

American Psychiatric Association. (2013). Substance related and addictive disorders. In *Diagnostic and statistical manual of mental disorders* (5th ed.). Washington, DC: Author.

Bless, J. J., Laroi, F., Latoyaux, J., Kompus, K., Krakvik, B., Vedul-Kjelsas, E., Kalhovde, A. M., & Hugdahl, K. (2018). Do adverse life events at first onset of auditory verbal hallucinations influence subsequent voice characteristics? Results from an epidemiological study. *Psychiatry Research, 261*, 232–236.

Cisler, J. M., & Koster, E. H. (2010). Mechanisms of attentional biases towards threat in anxiety disorders: An integrative review. *Clinical Psychology Review, 30*(2), 203–216.

Dodgson, G., & Gordon, S. (2009). Avoiding false negatives: Are some auditory hallucinations an evolved design flaw? *Behavioural and Cognitive Psychotherapy, 37*, 325–334.

Falip, M., Carreño, M., Donaire, A., Maestro, I., Pintor, L., Bargalló, N., Boget, T., Raspall, A., Rumià, J., & Setoaín, J. (2009). Postictal psychosis: a retrospective study in patients with refractory temporal lobe epilepsy. *Seizure, 18*(2), 145–149.

Ford, J. M., & Mathalon, D. H. (2005). Corollary discharge dysfunction in schizophrenia: Can it explain auditory hallucinations? *International Journal of Psychophysiology, 58*(2–3), 179–189.

Garwood, L., Dodgson, G., Bruce, V., & McCarthy-Jones, S. (2015). A preliminary investigation into the existence of a hypervigilance subtype of auditory hallucination in people with psychosis. *Behavioral and Cognitive Psychotherapy, 43*(1), 52–62.

Irwin, L. G., & Fortune, D. G. (2014). Risks factors for psychosis secondary to temporal lobe epilepsy: A systematic review. *The Journal of Neuropsychiatry and Clinical Neurosciences, 26*, 5–23.

Jones, S. R. (2010). Do we need multiple models of auditory verbal hallucinations? Examining the phenomenological fit of cognitive and neurological models. *Schizophrenia Bulletin, 36*(1), 566–575.

McCarthy-Jones, S., & Resnick, P. J. (2014). Listening to voices: The use of phenomenology to differentiate malingered from genuine auditory verbal hallucinations. *International Journal of International of Law and Psychiatry, 37*(2), 183–189.

McCarthy-Jones, S., Trauer, T., Mackinnon, A., Sims, E., Thomas, N., & Copolov, D. L. (2014). A new phenomenological survey of auditory hallucinations: Evidence for subtypes and implications for theory and practice. *Schizophrenia Bulletin, 40*(1), 231–235.

Sachdev, P. S. (1998). Schizophrenia-like psychosis and epilepsy: The status of the association. *American Journal of Psychiatry, 155*(3), 325–336.

Shea, S. C. (2011). *The practical art of suicide assessment: A guide for mental health professionals and substance abuse counselors*. Lexington, KY: Mental Health Presses.

Speth, J., Frenzel, C., & Voss, U. (2013). A differentiating empirical linguistic analysis of dreamer activity in reports of EEG-controlled REM-dreams and hypnagogic hallucinations. *Consciousness and Cognition, 22*, 1013–1021.

Waters, F., Dirk Blom, J., Thanh Dang-Vu, T., Cheyne, A. J., Alderson-Day, B., Woodruff, P., & Collerton, D. (2016). What is the link between hallucinations, dreams, and hypnagogic-hypnopompic experiences? *Schizophrenia Bulletin, 42*(5), 1098–1109.

5

FLEXIBILITY

Promoting Flexibility Sets the Tone

> *Reflection: Where do you catch yourself being rigid in how you have run groups in the past? Where/how have you been flexible as a group leader, and how can you make improvements?*

The "culture" of my Wednesday Voices and Visions group is unlike any other group I have encountered at my agency. Some days it seems like a classic therapy group—people sitting around a circle and discussing their mental health-related concerns. However, a lot of times the group discussions weave between discussions about coffee, *voices and visions,* group members' social lives, *trauma and stigma,* and (the grand finale) an impromptu group sing-along/line dancing session. I have worked hard to create a group culture in which flexibly allows people to express their wonderful, quirky, serious, silly selves. Why do this for a voices group? Because talking about ones' voices and visions can be scary, embarrassing, and intimidating.

When I was hospitalized as a psychiatric patient, my fellow clients DID NOT talk about their psychosis-related experiences in group, or even during meals or smoke breaks. Admissions about "hallucinations" were generally whispered amongst us in quiet moments before bed, or during moments of insomnia at 2 in the morning. In those moments, fellow clients and I spoke of our awareness that sharing the fullness of our extreme state experiences would likely keep us "locked up." From talking with the psychiatrists where I was an inpatient, "hearing voices" was akin to being "locked up." I was not homicidal or suicidal. Just hearing voices and having visions. My hearing voices group clients echo this same sentiment when they share their experiences. Sharing the full details of their lived experiences left them feeling vulnerable and wide open to judgment from medical staff, friends, and family.

The group facilitators with whom I spoke, and my own lived experience, has taught me that cultivating a group environment of open-mindedness and flexibility encourages clients to view themselves and their voices in a less rigid and judgmental manner. Therefore, I wanted to create a safe, authentic, non-judgmental, and welcoming space for clients to be themselves, openly share their lived experiences, and discover that life with voices doesn't have to be scary (or too serious). Dillon and Hornstein's (2013) observations on effective hearing voices groups also support this data. They indicate that facilitators should take a "relaxed" approach, be "non-judgmental," and remain open-minded about group members' viewpoints regarding their experiences. These researchers stated, "because there is not judgment … for the first time in their lives [group members] can reveal what is happening inside them" (p. 290). Studies on clients' experiences in hearing voices groups also support the importance of being non-judgmental, but did not specifically mention the term "flexibility" as a mechanism of change (Goodliffe, Hayward, Brown, Turton, & Dannahy, 2010; Newton, Larkin, Melhuish, & Wykes, 2007).

Singing with Sophie

Recently, new clients from a group home had been attending my Voices & Visions group, and several long-term group members (read: two-year attendees) had recently moved on. A new "normal" was being created, as the exiting group members had a big group presence, and the new members were not familiar with attending a group that directly addressed their voices, visions, and unusual perceptions/beliefs. Up until recently, group attendees' diagnoses ranged from acute psychotic disorder, bipolar with psychotic features, and depression with psychotic features. Still other group members attended because they were looking for a safe place to discuss their spiritual experiences, such as mediumship, talking with angels, or being a prophet in their church community. The newer members all appeared to have difficulty with both positive *and* negative symptoms of their schizophrenia or schizoaffective disorders. Having these folks attend group was fantastic, because they could use the time to improve social skills, which may have deteriorated due to the increased presence of alogia, decreased emotional expression, low energy, and voices/visions. Based upon clients' reported interests, I began weaving movement-based activities into group, which encouraged emotional expression and group bonding. All the clients indicated they enjoyed music—singing, listening, and playing it. Therefore, group sing-alongs became a common practice (with a little help from our enthusiastic "lead vocalist," 75-year-old Miss Sophie, who was diagnosed with schizophrenia disorder). Weekly, with little prompting, she would ask, "can we sing now?" She would then pop up and lead the group in rousing versions of popular country songs such as "The Gambler" and "Country Roads Take Me Home"—complete with dance moves! At first, group members would only look on and smile, but her enthusiasm was so infectious, we all began to join in, tapping and clapping to the music. Singing with Sophie also became a way for group members to "take a breather" from intense topics such as past hospitalizations, the stigma and shame of voices/visions, and coping with paranoia. There are also several enthusiastic dancers in the group (including myself), so sometimes I pull up the Electric Slide or Boot Scootin' Boogie on my phone (nothing too provocative or triggering), and the group will line dance. Those unable to dance are encouraged to clap along or use the percussion instruments provided in the group room, such as maracas or tambourines.

During one such dance party, one of the clients, Connor, who had a diagnosis of schizophrenia and was ordinarily stoic throughout group, began laughing, and pulled a throw blanket out "matador style" to corral the enthusiastic dancers. (An overzealous Miss Sophie was trying to twerk in front of a much younger client, and Connor's matador moves brought this to a quick end.) Then we all sat down, resumed the discussion about paranoia, and finished up group.

Discussing behavioral activation and social skills, while helpful, doesn't always compare to the real thing! Clients who experience voices and visions often meet criteria for schizophrenia spectrum disorders, and researchers have discovered this client population demonstrates deficits in coordinating their body movements with interaction partners (e.g., nonverbal synchrony) (Condon & Ogston, 1966; Kupper, Ramseyer, Hoffmann, & Tschacher, 2015; Raffard, Salesse, Marin, Del-Monte, Schmidt, Varlet et al., 2015; Varlet, Marin, Raffard, Schmidt, Capdevielle, Boulenger et al., 2012). Coordinated movement activities, whether small (e.g., finger tapping) or broad (e.g., group dance party), have been empirically proven to promote social bonding and cooperative behavior (Valdesolo & Desteno, 2011; Tarr, Launay, & Dunbar, 2014).

It is important to keep in mind that clients who hear voices often have trauma histories (as mentioned in a previous chapter) in which their fear-based response is to shut down, fight, or attempt to escape. If the bio-emotional reactions to trauma leave long-lasting imprints, PTSD symptoms may occur. However, "dance, movement, and rhythm are activities that provide an immediate resource to shift physiological states … these state-shifts even if momentary can be metaphorically perceived as momentary 'threads' that can weave a tapestry of restoration, healing, and reconnection" (Gray, 2017, p. 44). In an interview about trauma and the brain, Dr. Bruce Perry, a psychiatrist and researcher, explained that folks with developmental trauma are likely to experience *some* disorganization in the lower parts of their brains such as the brainstem and diencephalon (MacKinnon, 2012). (For those neuro nerds like me, the brainstem controls the flow of sensory messages in the brain and manages basic body functions like breathing, blood pressure, consciousness, swallowing, etc. The diencephalon acts like a messenger by relaying sensory info between brain regions and controls many functions in the autonomic nervous system. The brain's stress-response systems originate in these two structures.; Donnelly, 2017; Mohn, 2017.) Perry explains that in order to change a disorganized neural network in the brain, we need to engage in bottom-up processing involving repetitive patterned activity. He suggested using repetitive therapeutic interventions like dancing (!!!), grooming a horse, massage, swinging, or drumming to influence the brainstem directly, assist in neural reorganization, and ultimately promote improved regulation of the body. Plus, these activities are so much fun for group bonding (Mackinnon, 2012).

Additionally, other researchers are exploring the use of movement-based interventions in group settings to address trauma symptoms (which all my group members report having), including sensorimotor psychotherapy, drumming, Eye Movement Desensitization Reprocessing (EMDR), and dance therapy (Dunphy, Elton, & Jordan, 2014; Gonzalez-Vazquez, Rodriguez-Lago, Seoane-Pillado, Fernandez, Garcia-Guerrero, & Santed-German, 2018; Langmuir, Kirsh, & Classen, 2012; Perkins, Ascenso, Atkins, Fancourt, & Williamon, 2016). Instead of talking about behavioral synchrony, or suggesting clients sign up for a dance or drumming circle, group members and I engage them in movement-based interventions in a group. This gives folks the opportunity to try out dance, drumming, and other activities in an environment in which they feel safe and supported, and it also encourages group member bonding. Plus—although this information is anecdotal, I have observed my group members more openly share difficult information about their voices and visions after our mid-group dance breaks or sing-alongs.

The Group Room

Folks who experience voices often come from environments in which they had no control over where they moved, sat, ate, or slept. Therefore, I and many of the facilitators with whom I spoke stress the importance of flexible group room seating.

> *I do like the circle … However, maybe it could be intimidating for some people, so I feel like there needs to be some other option. I think talking about voices can be very scary. I think sometimes people want to be able to listen and maybe they need to work up the courage to talk. I think options are important for them—for people who have different styles of relating.*

When new group members show up for the first time in my groups, they often prefer to sit against the wall. Although I invite them to join the circle, I do not force the issue, and I make sure to include them in any discussion which occurs in the room. Awhile back, there was a regular group member, Barb, a woman in her 50s, who would always sit with her back to the wall, woolen hat pulled down around her ears (even in summer), and jacket zipped up to her chin. The group respected Barb's decision to sit by the wall and never seemed to question her seating choices. Throughout her attendance in the group, I would always make a point of greeting her and encouraging her to participate in the group discussions. Over time, Barb began to open up about her lived experiences with voices and visions—just a little bit.

Don't Be Too Teachy!

Half the respondents with whom I spoke indicated that facilitators should avoid being "too rigid," "authoritarian," or "too teachy." One facilitator explained:

> *Ineffective interventions would be tough love. I've never seen that work with this population. Other ineffective interventions would be being overly confrontational. If you're overly confrontational you are mimicking or recreating or potentially recreating the environment that caused them to be psychotic.*

I have witnessed facilitators who run their groups like a high school classroom, which never seems to inspire a free-flowing discussion of topics. When I come into the group room, I generally have a topic or "game plan" about where I hope to guide the group discussion, but this plan may be placed on the back burner if group members become engaged in other topics. I do steer group members away from controversial topics such as politics (e.g., "You can talk about *the president/elections/immigration* after group—let's refocus on what Todd was saying about feeling safe.").

Many of the folks who attend my group do not like too many handouts or worksheets for various reasons (e.g., too much like school, vision problems, difficulties reading), so I limit my use of these tools. Also, clients often hand them back to me after group saying, "I won't use this" and/or "I don't need it." Additionally, I have watched group members become caught up in reading the handout or filling out the worksheet, and their focus moves away from connecting with fellow group members. Too much worksheet/handout time seems to slow down the flow of my group members' conversations.

A favorite intervention of mine is asking group members, "By a show of hands, how many of you have experienced: *a certain medication side effect/mental health-related stigma scenario/particular type of voice or vision*?" I raise my own hand if the experience is something I have encountered as well. The group members always seem to appreciate my candor. They may ask a few questions about my experience, and I will briefly share if the information seems clinically appropriate. The technique allows an experience to be normalized by other group members, often gets them asking one another about symptoms, and makes the process more group member focused. This intervention once led to a very eye-opening discussion by several group members about how psychosis-related symptoms were managed in some hospitals and prisons.

Case Example: Betty and Bob

During one particular group session, conversation had dried up with no one sharing any experiences. This particular cluster of group members had been working together for approximately a month, seemed to feel comfortable with one another, and had already traded personal stories about psychosis-related symptoms. I knew over half the group members had been hospitalized at our clinic's crisis unit or the local inpatient psychiatric unit, and I believed they would benefit from sharing past treatment stories. So I launched into my "show of hands" intervention to normalize psychiatric stays, which can often feel very stigmatizing, isolating, and embarrassing, "Show of hands—myself included—how many of you have been hospitalized for hearing voices?" All the hands went up. "Were your experiences helpful, not helpful, God-awful, or what?"

Two group members, Betty and Bob, who both had spent time in state hospitals and prison, began discussing horrible restraints and "the hood," which staff used to prohibit clients from spitting or biting. Both clients thought they had been the only person they knew who had experienced the shameful "hood," and commiserated with one another about their awful experiences. Had I simply given the clients a worksheet or handout listing possible horrible experiences and had clients go around the circle reading the handout, an organic discussion may not have flowed so freely. I believe handouts (used sparingly) can be useful, but over-reliance on such tools does not seem to be a crowd pleaser with my group members.

Psychological Versus Spiritual

Many of the group facilitators with whom I spoke believe in the importance of being open-minded, or at the very least flexible about their beliefs regarding the etiology of psychosis-related symptoms in their clients. As I mentioned in the previous chapter on safety, researchers have not uncovered a definitive reason for what causes voice hearers, both clinical and non-clinical folks, to have their unique sensory experiences (McCarthy-Jones & Resnick, 2014). Therefore, being staunchly wedded to a certain reason(s) for a client's voice hearing experiences seems short-sighted. Years ago, while reading a debate about voice hearing on the ISPS message boards, multiple clinicians became embroiled in a heated debate about the phenomenology of voice hearing. Some people were anti-medical model and believed voices were a spiritual experience. Others were staunch supporters of the medical model and believed voices were strictly a psychiatric phenomenon. A psychiatrist, who had been in the field for 20-plus years, shared what became my favorite point of view about the merits of incorporating both points of view (medical and spiritual) in one's conceptualization. I paraphrase, but basically the psychiatrist indicated that looking at each point of view individually was like looking through one lens of a pair of binoculars at a time. Only when we look through both lenses simultaneously can we obtain the fullest picture.

While explaining what goals and objectives they develop for their groups, two of the facilitators I interviewed stated:

> *The main goal is to validate that there is a lot of meanings that people can make of experiences, and that there is no one right stance … it's a really complicated matter, and there are a lot of truths out there.*
>
> *I see it very much as a stance of non-pathology. A stance of not equating voice hearing with schizophrenia or even with psychosis. But allowing spiritual reasons, just the differences in the way people think, just kind of allowing people to talk about it from their own perspective rather than sort of an illness model.*

Another facilitator, who works with clients with a Maori cultural background, also uses a spiritual framework with her clients. She and her co-facilitator encourage their group members to discuss spiritual and cultural reasons for the development of voices, visions, and unusual beliefs. They regularly bring in "Maori cultural advisors" to help their clients understand their experiences from the perspective of their indigenous culture.

> *We brought in a session on different perspectives like Maori cultural perspective, or shamanism, other ways of thinking about the*

> *voice hearing experience other than the medical kind, other than as an illness.*

Recently, I came across a study published in *PLOS One*, a peer-reviewed scientific journal, in which researchers explored the differences in brain activity between psychic mediums and a control group (Fernando Peres, Moreira-Almeida, Caixeta, Leao, & Newberg, 2012). Researchers had two groups of psychic mediums ("expert" and "less expert") engage in a psychography task "in which allegedly 'the spirit writes through the medium's hand' for potential alterations in cerebral activity" (Fernando Peres, Moreira-Almeida, Caixeta, Leao, & Newberg, 2012, p. 1) These subjects' writing samples were then compared to those of the sample control group—non-psychic mediums, whose brains were also monitored. Researchers used single photon emission computed tomography to assess both groups. They discovered the experienced psychographers displayed lower levels of brain activity in brain areas related to cognitive processing compared to the control group. Interestingly, the average complexity scores of the writings of the experienced psychographers were higher than the control group. The researchers argued, "relaxation seems an unlikely explanation for the under activation of brain areas specifically related to the cognitive processing being carried out" (Fernando Peres, Moreira-Almeida, Caixeta, Leao, & Newberg, 2012, p. 7). Although this is an exploratory study, these researchers' work bears mentioning.

When clients share spiritual experiences with me in group, I often use the "binocular" approach (one lens spiritual and one medical) to inform my reactions. However, some "spirity experiences" (as I have deemed them over the years) I hear about cannot be explained in psychological or medical terms. (Truth be told, some experiences I have encountered over the years defy logic.) I remain open to the possibility that some voices and visions have otherworldly origins—consider Jesus, Joan of Arc, and Gandhi. They were famous voice hearers who reported connecting with a higher power and did some pretty amazing things. So when clients ask me, "Andrea, do you think I really did connect with my father/spirit guides/God/an angel/a demon," I reply, "Anything is possible. Let's talk about it!" Quickly shutting down a client based upon their unusual perceptions or beliefs only serves to isolate him or her—which is the opposite of what I hope to achieve in group.

Dead or Alive

Mr. John, a 50-something Caucasian male, is a frequent guest on my clinic's crisis unit and at the various local psychiatric inpatient facilities around the area. He has a diagnosis of schizoaffective disorder, and reports "being dead but alive and rotting," although his body remains unblemished and intact. This type of rare neuropsychiatric condition is also known as Cotard delusion, in which the person believes they are a walking corpse. The etiology of this particular somatic delusion remains unclear, and there is limited research on Cotard delusion because the condition is rarely seen. When Mr. John does present himself for services on the crisis unit, he will report being non-compliant with his anti-psychotic medications. He also reports remaining isolated in his home with his wife, who is his primary support person. After Mr. John remains on the crisis unit for a week, spending time with fellow group members, eating and sleeping at regular intervals, and remaining compliant with medications, the intensity of his symptoms decreases and he is (naturally) less scared, angry, and anxious. He can then joke around about his symptoms (e.g., John laughingly agreed with me once that, yes, duct tape *would be* an acceptable intervention if any of his fingers rotted off) and explore possible ways to cope in a healthy way with symptoms. However, John becomes very shut down emotionally when talking with some of the staff who are not flexible with how they approach his Cotard delusion. When a medical staff member insisted John say, "I am only feeling dead on the inside but alive on the outside," I watched his shoulders slump and his face switch from animated to blank.

Now, as a general rule, I do not believe in zombies, and recognized that Mr. John meets criteria for Cotard delusion. He comes to the clinic infrequently, so staff do not have a solid and emotionally safe connection with Mr. John. Therefore, challenging him about the validity of his delusion would not be my immediate approach with Mr. John. Meet him where he's at! Ideally, his staff should work together to formulate the best plan of action when working with him. Having a rogue member of the team denounce his lived experience does not breed emotional safety. Instead, as suggested by multiple therapeutic approaches developed for this client population (e.g., Cognitive Behavioral Therapy for Psychosis, Compassion Focused Therapy for Psychosis, Pre-Therapy), building rapport with Mr. John and developing an empathic understanding of his frame of reference would be the first couple of objectives. Mr. John knows he responds well to medications and that they decrease the intensity of his symptoms. Medical staff should work together to find the appropriate doses of medications to help his symptoms become more manageable. Down the road, Mr. John may be able to explore evidence against his unusual beliefs (especially since they are ego-dystonic) and generate alternative explanations.

Many of my group members (past and present) reported having similar experiences with mental health professionals. Although Mr. John was not a group member, I mention this particular case because experiences like his often lead folks who have voices, visions, and unusual beliefs to avoid seeking out treatment for fear the staff will discount their lived experiences. Therefore, clinical situations like Mr. John's underscore the importance of remaining flexible in how one approaches a client with voices, visions, or unusual beliefs.

Meeting People Where They Are

Talking about voices and visions in a group of people is intimidating and makes clients uncomfortable. Some clients who join the group "hit the ground running" and discuss their extreme state experiences immediately. As a former voice hearer, I refused to open up about my extreme state experiences with most people in my life after being hospitalized. I wanted to put the experience behind me, tuck it in my mental closet, and move forward with my life. As I mentioned earlier, attending the ISPS conference in New York City, listening to other voice hearers there discuss their experiences, and speaking with group facilitators inspired me to "come out" as someone with lived voice hearing experiences to colleagues and clients. Not everyone is so lucky, and I remain flexible about allowing group members to share and participate in group at their own pace. The longer-term group members and myself model open discussions about voice hearing to newer and more reticent members. I also utilize different types of interventions to encourage sharing.

Case Example: Jenny and Art Interventions

One of my group members, Jenny, disclosed during her treatment plan meeting how challenging talking in group settings is for her. However, she reported enjoying attending the hearing voices group and learning a lot from fellow group members. I began noticing how much Jenny drew pictures while the group engaged in discussions, so I asked to see what she was drawing one day after group. Jenny showed me an intricate drawing of how she conceptualized her trauma and voices. Inspired, I asked Jenny if instead of talking in group—for now—she would like to draw her responses to group discussions and show me after group. She agreed. The group members began asking to see Jenny's drawings, and sharing these drawings with the group is a way of inviting members into Jenny's "world." She remains reticent about being a large contributor (verbally) in group, but her presence is felt by the group through her art. I typically ask Jenny follow-up questions about her art pieces, such as:

- How did the group discussion influence this drawing?
- Tell me about what's going on in this drawing? (I never make initial interpretations but let the client tell me about the drawing.)

- Are your voices influencing anything in this drawing or somehow represented on this paper?

(It helps that I have a background in art therapy, but I have listed some great art therapy resources at the end of this chapter in case you don't! Art therapy interventions can be an effective way to explore scary topics, because the client has control of the content on the page and how much they verbalize about the content to the viewers—like therapists and fellow group members.)

There are a few clients in my therapy group who remain ambivalent about participating. They attend regularly, appear to be engaged in active listening, and appear to empathize via body language with fellow group members' stories. When asked directly by myself or fellow group members to discuss their extreme state experiences, these members demur. I'm okay with their reticence and hold out hope that these members will eventually feel safe enough to openly share their stories. However, if they never share a single story and benefit simply by listening, I'm fine with that too. Mental health can be achieved in a variety of ways—there is no one route to feeling better.

Summary Points

- Creating a group culture that embraces flexibility can allow people to be more open and expressive. An environment of open-mindedness and flexibility encourages clients to view themselves and their voices in a less rigid and less judgmental manner.
- Coordinated movement activities (such as finger tapping, dancing, etc.) can help promote social bonding and provide an opportunity for clients to shift physiological states, which can provide some relief for them, particularly when they have trauma histories, which many do.
- In setting up the group room, consider applying flexibility to allow for options in where clients sit. Some prefer to sit in a group circle, but others may find it more comfortable for

them to sit with their back to the wall, or to sit outside of the group and participate from a distance.

- Remember that Hearing Voices groups are not classroom settings. Avoid being too rigid or too authoritarian in your approach. Being overly confrontational also will not establish a safe-feeling group setting. While you may have a topic or general plan for a group meeting, it's helpful to be flexible enough to shift when group members have other priorities.
- Handouts can be helpful but should be used sparingly, as they may distract from the group process if overused.
- Be open-minded about the etiology of voices and visions (whether medical or spiritual) to allow for client experience and respect cultural beliefs and practices.
- Meet clients where they are. Having the flexibility to accept where a client is and allow them to be there without judgment can be helpful in making clients feel more comfortable and accepted.

A Few Art Therapy Resources

Folks in voices groups are often self-conscious about talking about voices, visions, and unusual beliefs. However, having them draw these experiences and/or thoughts related to them is often a less threatening option. Yes, there will be some conscientious objectors to these tasks, but for the most part the adults in my groups participate (and like the activities more than they originally thought).

Handbook of Art Therapy, *Second Edition, Cathy Malchiodi, 2011*

A great overview of art therapy that lists practical interventions and approaches for children, adults, and groups. This book includes a variety of theoretical approaches for art therapy (CBT, Humanistic, Psychoanalytic) and is a classic book in the field. The interventions in this gem show how art therapy techniques can be applied to "traditional" theoretical approaches. I do not believe one particular theoretical orientation is the magic road to healing for voice hearers. The group leaders I spoke with all had different theoretical orientations. Use evidence-based practice guidelines: if you can find research to support your approach to working with voice hearers, the clients respond well, and the skills needed to carry out the interventions are within your wheelhouse (clinically), then GO FOR IT (APA Presidential Task Force, 2006).

Raising Self Esteem in Adults: An Eclectic Approach with Art Therapy, CBT, and DBT Techniques, First Edition, Susan Buchalter, 2015

This book has practical interventions based upon concepts of CBT, DBT, and mindfulness. The people in my voices groups often struggle with issues around worthlessness, so I am always a fan of activities that promote self-confidence.

The CBT Art Activity Book: 100 Illustrated Handouts for Creative Therapeutic Work, Jennifer Guest, 2015

This book is full of worksheets that fuse art therapy, charming Zentangle-type illustrations that can be colored!, and CBT concepts. The worksheets address topics such as self-esteem, emotions, change and loss, anger management, and problem-solving. There may be people in group who may be intimidated by drawing, so this book allows them to color (a relaxing activity and helpful distraction technique) and/or fill in the worksheets with simple drawings. The CBT aspect of this book can be fused with CBTp concepts, and the coloring sheets can help strengthen folks' ability to engage in a mindful task (in a playful way).

References

American Psychological Association Presidential Task Force on Evidence Based Practice. (2006). Evidence-based practice in psychology. *American Psychologist, 61*, 271–285.

Condon, W., & Ogston, W. (1966). Sound film analysis of normal and pathological behavior patterns. *Journal of Nervous and Mental Disease, 143*, 338–47.

Dillon, J., & Hornstein, G. A. (2013). Hearing voices peer support groups: A powerful alternative for people in distress. *Psychosis, 5*(3), 286–295.

Donnelly, L. (2017). Physiology: The brain: Function divisions. Anaesthesia & intensive care. *Medicine, 18*, 264–269.

Dunphy, K., Elton, M., & Jordan, A. (2014). Exploring dance/movement therapy in post-conflict Timor-Leste. *American Journal of Dance Therapy, 36*, 189–208.

Fernando Peres, J., Moreira-Almeida, A., Caixeta, L., Leao, F., & Newberg, A. (2012). Neuroimaging during trance state: A contribution to the study of dissociation. *PLOS One, 7*(11), pE49360.

Goodliffe, L., Hayward, M., Brown, D., Turton, W., & Dannahy, L. (2010). Group person-based cognitive therapy for distressing voices: Views from the hearers. *Psychotherapy Research, 20*(4), 447–461.

Gonzalez-Vazquez, A. I., Rodriguez-Lago, L., Seoane-Pillado, M. T., Fernandez, I., Garcia-Guerrero, F., & Santed-German, M. A. (2018). The progressive approach to EMDR group therapy for complex trauma and dissociation: A case-control study. *Frontiers in Psychology, 8*, 2377.

Gray, A. E. L. (2017). Polyvagal-informed dance/movement therapy for trauma: A global perspective. *American Journal of Dance Therapy, 1*, 43–46.

Kupper, Z., Ramseyer, F., Hoffmann, H., & Tschacher, W. (2015). Nonverbal synchrony in social interactions of patients with schizophrenia indicates socio-communicative deficits. *PLOS One, 10*(12), pE0145882.

Langmuir, J. I., Kirsh, S. G., & Classen, C. C. (2012). A pilot study of body-oriented group psychotherapy: Adapting sensorimotor psychotherapy for the group treatment of trauma. *Psychological Trauma: Theory, Research, Practice, and Policy, 4*(2), 214–226.

Mackinnon, L. (2012). The neurosequential model of therapeutics: An interview with Bruce Perry. *The Australian and New Zealand Journal of Family Therapy, 33*(3), 210–218.

McCarthy-Jones, S., & Resnick, P. J. (2014). Listening to voices: The use of phenomenology to differentiate malingered from genuine auditory verbal hallucinations. *International Journal of Law & Psychiatry, 37*(2), 183–189.

Mohn, E. (2017). *Brain stem.* Salem Press Encyclopedia of Health. Retrieved from http://proxy.myunion.edu/login?url=https://search.ebscohost.com/login.aspx?direct=true&db=ers&AN=89403907&site=eds-live&scope=site

Newton, E., Larkin, M., Melhuish, R., & Wykes, T. (2007). More than just a place to talk: Young people's experiences of group psychological therapy as an early intervention for auditory hallucinations. *Psychology & Psychotherapy: Theory, Research & Practice, 80*(1), 127–149.

Perkins, R., Ascenso, S., Atkins, L., Fancourt, D., & Williamon, A. (2016). Making music for mental health: How group drumming mediates recovery. *Psychology of Well-being: Theory, Research, & Practice, 6*(1), 1–17.

Tarr, B., Launay, J., & Dunbar, R. I. M. (2014). Music and social bonding: "Self-other" merging and neurohormonal mechanisms. *Frontiers in Psychology: Auditory Cognitive Neuroscience*, *5*, 1–10.

Valdesolo, P., & Desteno, D. (2011). Synchrony and the social tuning of compassion. *Emotion*, *11*(2), 262–6.

Varlet, M., Marin, L., Raffard, S., Schmidt, R. C., Capdevielle, D., Boulenger, J., Del-Monte, J., & Bardy, B. G. (2012). Impairments of social motor coordination in schizophrenia. *PLos ONE*, *7*(1), 1–8.

6

USE OF GROUP PROCESS TO FOSTER HEALTHY ATTACHMENTS

Language, Style, Humor, and Other Tips

> *Reflection: Imagine being in the shoes of the client in a Hearing Voices Group. What would be your concerns? What would you want from the group facilitator in order to help you get the most benefit from the group? What if it was a loved one in the group—what would you want for him/her?*

For most clients, stepping into a hearing voices group is an acknowledgment that their voices have become overwhelming, are not going away anytime soon, and/or cannot be ignored. Owning up to having extreme state experiences can understandably provoke a great deal of shame, fear, sadness, and/or worry. There are many reasons for this. In Western society, there is a great deal of stigma attached to these experiences. Prior to attending group, clients have seldom shared their experiences or told others about their voices or visions. Clients who open up to family, friends, or mental health professionals (myself included) are often cautious to not share too much detail for fear of hospitalization.

"Am I in Trouble?"

I have a client, Al, a 41-year-old Caucasian male, who punctuates every disclosure in the hearing voices group with, "Am I in trouble?" At first I thought he was joking, but I quickly learned he was NOT. Al genuinely worried that the sheriff or orderlies from the local mental hospital were waiting nearby to involuntarily hospitalize him. Due to struggles with managing his schizophrenia-related symptoms and drug addiction, Al had been hospitalized countless times. He lived in constant fear of saying something about his voices or symptoms that would land him back in an inpatient unit.

According to the facilitators with whom I spoke, my experiences as a facilitator, and my own lived experience, most of the clients who attend voices groups have trauma histories and find it difficult to articulate their emotions. Consequently, attending to group process is an important method of engaging clients' emotional processing as they explore their experiences. I have listed in the following pages concepts to keep in mind when running groups specifically for voice hearers. These bits of wisdom are gathered from talking with other hearing voices facilitators from around the world, my own experiences running such groups, and personal thoughts as a former voice hearer.

Language Used

Talking about voices, visions, and other extreme state experiences in front of others is challenging and often leaves clients feeling vulnerable, scared, and uncertain. Many struggle with alexithymia and have difficulty noticing and articulating how voices impact them emotionally. I have taken to describing this experience as the "yarn ball of emotion—each string a different thought or emotion." This metaphor is well-received by clients and illustrates the importance of language as a tool to connect clients and the facilitator. I have made the mistake (and seen other well-meaning facilitators do the same) of using language that is too clinical or formal too soon, which can cause the entire group to shut down (e.g., stop talking, look away, ignore each other). Not surprisingly, many of the facilitators with whom I spoke encouraged group leaders to use relatable language when talking with clients about their experiences. *Not because clients cannot understand the terminology*—but because using relatable metaphors, concepts, or words to describe voices or visions makes them less scary. In all the interviews I did with expert facilitators, I noticed that no one used the terms "visual hallucinations," "psychosis," "paranoia," or "auditory hallucinations." Instead, they describe people's experiences with words like "voices and visions," "extreme state experiences," and/or "unusual beliefs." I have been known to ask clients if their voices are "nice, mean, or sassy?", which frequently elicits smiles all around from group members. Additionally, using everyday words and phrases to describe clients' experiences is more normalizing and less pathologizing. We as mental health providers are often tasked with socializing folks to therapy, and I have found clients are more at ease when I use language which is closer to their everyday speech. Words/phrases I tend to avoid when talking to clients:

- Cognitions (I just say "thoughts")
- Ideation (I typically ask, "Have you thought about killing yourself or hurting yourself" or "do you think others are trying to hurt/kill you" instead of asking about suicidal or paranoid ideation.)
- Hallucinations (Instead I say, "voices or visions")
- Suspicious (I usually ask, "Do you have a tough time trusting others beyond what you feel is reasonable?")
- Acting psychotic (I prefer precision of language, and my skin crawls when I hear another mental health professional say a client is "acting psychotic" or "presenting with psychotic features." Be specific with your words—what exactly are you seeing clinically? Is the client hearing voices, experiencing paranoia, speaking in a disorganized manner? Choose your words carefully and wield them respectfully.)
- Any word that could show up on an SAT exam

It's not because I think clients are dummies who can't handle hearing big words or clinical terms—they certainly can. Think of times when you had to speak with a surgeon or auto mechanic—never fun times, and often anxiety-provoking. These people may toss around words which to them are commonplace, like rhinorrhea or torque. Yes, we can look them up (thank you Google), but it's more helpful to hear a simpler version of the terms: runny nose or twisting force. My point is, keep the language simple so people can focus on the content of what you say and not trip over fancy clinical language.

Facilitator Style

Many facilitators with whom I spoke discouraged rushing group process because progress with this population often moves at a glacial pace. "Meeting clients where they are" is a phrase often bandied about in textbooks and during training supervision, but never is this tenet more important than when working with this client population! When I was experiencing my own extreme state experiences, I felt insulted and angry when family members and clinicians tried to "reassure me" that what I was hearing were not spirits of dead loved ones but hallucinations. Clients appreciate not having their experiences harshly questioned, corrected, or dismissed. Below are three clinician behaviors I have witnessed in co-facilitators, supervisees, and even (oops) myself which are especially unhelpful with this client population:

The Rusher

This facilitator peppers clients with questions about their voice hearing experiences with rapid-fire questions like a verbal machine gun. Ugh! As someone who has endured this type of experience as a client, I can assure you that talking with this type of therapist or psychiatrist made me nervous and twitchy. No sooner had I shared something deeply personal about how I perceived my voices than the clinician rushed in with the next comment:

Therapist: "Thankyouforsharingthat. (Briefest of pauses) Areyouhearingvoicesnow?"
Me: "Huh?"
Therapist: "Are ... you ... hear-ing ... voi-ces no-ow?"
Me: (*Thinking: Why should I tell this condescending fool anything?*) "Um no."

The Rusher's conversational style feels dismissive, and I have witnessed it shut down group discussions—*every-single-time*! When I have discussed this tendency to rush through questions during group sessions with my supervisees, or reflected on my own (not so great) responses to clients, anxiety is often a common theme. Students frequently have discomfort with voice hearing, anxiety about the client's state of mind ("please God no command suicidal or homicidal voices!"), and worries regarding how to best respond in a helpful way.

Rushing clients along with rapid-fire questions is usually not therapeutic because it leaves the recipient feeling drained and overwhelmed. We as facilitators do not want to provide or support this kind of experience in group because (as many of the facilitators with whom I spoke observed) feeling overwhelmed is what often leads clients to hear voices in the first place. As one facilitator noted:

> *I am cautious about being in a hurry. Because I know … this stuff does take time. People hanging out in relationship with folks … The experiences [of many clients] were so intense that they were flooded with emotion and they couldn't really process it, so it overwhelmed them. Sometimes … people are not able to take it in all at once … so things are not stored in coherent memory. There are pieces of memory or their metaphorical experiences of what happened … [or individuals sometimes experience] sadness that doesn't seem to be attached to anything.*

As a group leader, I let the statements clients make have time to land and settle into the space. Silence is an intervention too! Clients may be sharing about their experiences for the first time in a group, so even the act of speaking out loud is often therapeutic.

The Lecturer

Another common mistake I have observed is therapists lecturing at clients too much. This does not allow clients adequate time to discuss the material provided by the group facilitator, or to process what is currently on their minds. Clients who attend hearing voices groups are usually eager to talk about their experiences with others in a safe environment. Many report coming out of families, jails, or hospitals where they were or still are lectured to by others. As a facilitator, I do not want to recreate negative experiences my group clients may have encountered in the community. Although I recognize the inherent power differential between myself and my clients, it is often important to "set it on the shelf" and relate to them as one human being to another. One of my mentors, Dr. Perry Stanley, always likes to say, "We have more in common with these people *we call clients* than differences." In the case of hearing voices groups, I can certainly relate to what my group members say! Whether or not you have experienced voices or visions yourself, as human beings, we all share common hopes, fears, and desires. To make space for human experience, I have learned to present the material (e.g., articles, handouts, etc.) in such a way as to encourage discussion. Group members read through handouts first and are then invited to reflect on certain sections of the material, or to discuss whether or not certain articles reflect their own experiences.

The Terrible Timing Facilitator

Timing is very crucial when running a group with clients who have voices and visions. Just showing up is an act of bravery, and I tell new attendees they can share as much or as little as they feel comfortable. Many (read: most) of the clients in my voice hearing groups have experienced boundary violations in their lives (physical, emotional, and/or mental), so I mindfully demonstrate healthy boundaries with group members. I have seen well-meaning group therapists ask pointed questions of clients with no sense of whether or not the clients seemed "ready" to provide answers. The therapists mistakenly seemed to feel the time was ripe to throw out personal or pointed questions, so they asked.

One of my group members delightfully made the following statement in my current voices and visions group: "Our stories are like poop. Hold them in and you're in pain. But if you let them out too fast—it's a big ol' mess!" (Perhaps only in the West Virginian clinic where I work can group process be so colorfully and honestly described.) Allow group clients to share at a pace comfortable to them. Observe non-verbals to ascertain if someone is "ok" with sharing more than a few thoughts or ideas. Verbal poking or prodding by the facilitator or by other group members to encourage a flow of information (no pun intended) often backfires.

Humor

One of my favorite parts about running my voices and visions groups is the humor and silliness which erupts during the conversations between clients and myself. I use gentle humor to poke fun at my own experiences as a former voice hearer, or to underscore a point I make during group discussions. This approach is intentional and encourages clients to view their own experiences (perhaps for the first time) with humor as well.

Once, a long-time group member excitedly shared with the group that she was being driven to the airport by her son in order to take a long-awaited trip to visit another family member. "I'm so excited to be riding in the car with [my son]! I get to hear *Road Rage* the entire time," she declared with earnest enthusiasm. Several of the group members appeared confused, and one group member, who was new to the group, spoke up, "What is *Road Rage*? Is that one of your voices?" Many of the group members began to nod in agreement and looked curious. The woman who was to be traveling laughed and said, "No! *Road Rage* is what I call my son's anger when he drives! It's not one of my voices. I just think hearing my son get angry at other drivers is funny!" We all had a good laugh with the client and ourselves for assuming *Road Rage* was a voice! Moments such as those allow clients to relax and ease the tension of discussing more serious topics such as voices, nasty medication side effects ("three cheers and a hearty huzzah for weight gain and drooling!"), and horrifying hospitalization-related experiences.

Clients often learn to use humor in a healthy way to cope with their voices and visions. My favorite all-time example occurred several years ago when I first started a hearing voices group at my current clinic. A group member shared, "I have aliens living in my chair and couch." I asked him how big these aliens were since it sounded like they were hiding within the couch cushions and chair seat. The client assured me they were small and he had not officially seen the aliens, "But they're there. I can sense them. They haven't talked to me, but I talk to them." I asked this client if he was nervous about having aliens in his home, and if they were friendly. He explained, "I tell them to be respectful of me and I'll be respectful of them. And I gave them candy because I figured they were hungry." I calmly looked at him and declared, "That was a very kind thing to do." At this point, the client's eyes lit up and he smiled, "I gave them Starburst … because I'm not without a sense of humor!" At this point, the client and the entire group burst out laughing.

Three years later, this client and I still laugh about this story, and he remains unsure whether or not aliens were living in his couch and chair. Maybe they were … candy is a great unifier. In this particular scenario, humor was used to cope with a potentially scary situation for the client. However, always remember, as any comic will tell you, humor is about timing. It should be utilized with care, because we do not want clients to perceive us as glib or that we are trivializing their concerns.

Curiosity Versus Voyeurism

Several years ago, I attended a workshop on trauma with Dr. Bessel Van der Kolk in which he cautioned therapists about becoming too "voyeuristic" when asking clients about their trauma-related experiences. He said therapists do not *necessarily* need to learn all the gory details about clients' trauma experiences for them to heal. This idea has stuck with me over the years as I have run groups with clients who have voices and visions—most of whom have trauma histories, as many of the facilitators with whom I spoke indicated. In cautioning therapists to not be voyeurs,

Dr. Van der Kolk validated my experience as a therapist who exercises caution when asking about clients' lives (particularly trauma histories and voices), but his comment also validated my experience as a former voice hearer.

When I first returned from the hospital after a ten-day stay (due to hearing voices), my family and friends were eager to know what happened and to hear all the details. Their interest felt a great deal like gossip at my expense. I know their concern was genuine, but I was not comfortable talking with anyone about my experiences with the voices at that point, or for months afterward. Thankfully, I later saw a therapist who did not push me to reveal too much about my voices, and who showed genuine curiosity about my experiences. This allowed me to ultimately share at a comfortable pace.

In my work running voice hearing groups, clients often echo my own experiences, expressing frustration about therapists who "are too nosy," "jumped into talking about my trauma way too soon," or "asked too many questions about my voices." Voice hearers in particular are reluctant to share about their experiences for fear of labels, scorn, or having experiences discounted as "that's just crazy" or "it's all in your head." I have witnessed therapists in clinical case conferences or consultation discussions whose eyes spark with an uncomfortably intense interest when a client's voices, visions, or history of trauma are mentioned. Furthermore, as a client, I experienced therapists' demeanor change from clinical detachment to jackal-like intensity as I outlined my mental health history regarding past voice hearing. Awkward and uncomfortable does not begin to describe how I used to feel when telling new psychiatrists or other mental health professionals about my voices. Therefore, I will pass along the very helpful piece of advice my colleague, Dr. Rielly, shared with me when I was a psychology intern, and which I have subsequently passed along to my supervisees:

> *Watch your face!!! We as therapists should always be aware of our body language in session with clients, and this includes our facial*

expressions. I am not advocating for group facilitators to appear zombie-like and affect-free. Simply be aware of what your face is communicating in the moment when clients share potentially embarrassing, sensitive, or intimate details about their voices or lives. You certainly don't want clients to feel like the chum during an Animal Planet Shark Week *segment every time they share about their lives.*

I have learned (and trust me, it took practice!) to keep my face relaxed and my tone matter of fact when responding to clients: "You're hearing voices? No kidding. Are they mean? Sassy? Or both?" For example, I have an unconscious habit of quirking my right eyebrow when I find something interesting. Sometimes I catch myself doing this but other times the darn eyebrow pops up on its own. A client recently asked me, "When your eyebrow pops up, is it because you think I'm strange or what I'm saying is weird?" I replied, "My eyebrow does that when I'm intrigued and curious." The client seemed to like this reply based upon her smile and relaxed expression. My point is, know your facial expressions. I have said in a previous chapter, "watch your face," because clients who hear voices are often sensitive folks and will be closely reading your facial expressions for any sign of rejection. I was lucky enough to have a client ask me outright about my "quirks" (ha-ha), but not all clients are so forthright. Consequently, I warn new clients about my brow habit so they aren't thrown off. You'll have to find what works for you as a therapist—authentic to your style. However, a non-anxious presence with a gentle degree of empathic curiosity goes a long way toward allowing clients to feel safe in sharing about their experiences.

Recognize Clients' Sense of Pride

The last point I want to mention is about the importance of acknowledging clients' sense of personal pride regarding their ability to better manage their symptoms, improved relationships with others, or increased insight. There might have been a time when I was quick to point out how much a client had grown or remind them of where they started ("Remember when you were really paranoid and nailing your windows shut—look how much you've grown personally!"). I gradually realized (based upon client responses and my own growth as a clinician) that this approach felt akin to my older relatives (I'm talking to *you*, Aunt Emily) greeting my teenage self with: "I remember when you used to play with your Barbies and NOW you're going off to college!"

I do believe in discussing progress with clients in group but have learned to be much more subtle about it. Clients in my voices groups respond well to questions that allow them to reflect upon their growth, such as: "What have you learned from attending this group?" or "Have you noticed any changes in how you manage your voices or other extreme state experiences?" Putting the conversational ball in the clients' court allows them to reflect upon their growth, and they often mention benefits or areas of growth which I had not considered. I've learned this approach also inspires group members to chime in with their observations about one another—which can be very powerful validation indeed. I stress this point because clients (and I include myself in this category) are often embarrassed about where they were symptom-wise when they first sought out services to address voices, visions, or other extreme state experiences. This is sensitive stuff, and statements about growth from ones' therapist may be perceived as inauthentic ("You're paid to say that"). However, genuine comments from fellow group members, or their own reflections regarding their growth, feel truer and more authentic.

Why Is Group Process So Important?

Several of the facilitators with whom I spoke indicated that attending to group process leads to fostering healthy attachments between group members. Connection to others is crucial because, as one facilitator indicated:

> *[Clients] may be uncertain as to whether or not they are themselves or they are their perceptual disturbances … I think a lot*

> *of them have extraordinarily large difficulties with maintaining secure attachments to folks or maintaining a secure attachment to themselves … Yeah, we wanted to facilitate attachment. Like being able to feel connected to other people. Have a sense of belonging, permanence in the lives of other people.*

The majority of group leaders that I talked with stated a good group outcome was when group members began to seek out people in the group or within their community (e.g., hospital, town, or prison) for support. Group leaders believe this process develops through cultivating healthy relationships within a group setting. One facilitator, who works with an all-male population within a forensic hospital, explained that he fosters the development of genuine connections amongst group members by role modeling authenticity, so clients can begin to form stronger and deeper relationships with one another or individuals outside the group:

> *It's just getting where guys can really bring their real selves into the room. So many people who are chronically psychotic don't trust … that process at all … You just need to be real. That's the most powerful tool in the room if [facilitators] can just come in with our heart and our soul and be our self and be comfortable with that. People are taking it in and regardless of how refined our clinical skills are if you can just be a real human being amongst other human beings that's a real potent impact.*

For my own part, I have grown more and more comfortable in my own skin over the years, which I believe translates into authenticity with clients. There was a time when I would NEVER have considered telling clients about my voice hearing past, but now—if done for therapeutic purposes (for the clients' benefit and not my own)—I'm cool with it. My group clients tell me they appreciate my candor about my past experiences, and that my willingness to share makes me more credible. Authenticity can come across in many ways—how we respond, our body language, the stories we share. As a fellow therapist recently observed, authenticity is about "being true to what you feel about a situation versus what you feel the situation calls for." Put simply: don't be something you're not. It's tiring, a waste of energy, and I have observed that my clients in voices and visions groups have fine-tuned b.s. detectors. Clients will call you out every time!

Summary Points

- Remember that many people are understandably cautious in disclosing or opening up about voices for fear of hospitalizations, judgment, etc.
- Language is an important tool to connect clients, facilitators, and experiences. Relatable language is helpful in making the voices or visions more relatable, less pathologizing, and less frightening. Instead of using clinical terms such as "visual hallucinations," "psychosis," or "auditory hallucinations," consider using phrases such as "voices and visions," "extreme state experiences," and "unusual beliefs."
- Meet clients where they are and be patient with the process. Avoid being The Rusher, The Lecturer, or The Timing Neglector.
- Humor, used appropriately by the facilitator and group members, can be a very helpful tool and a healthy coping strategy within the group setting.
- When discussing trauma-related experiences, demonstrate curiosity without being voyeuristic. Be aware of facial expressions and body language and what you are communicating to clients particularly as they discuss sensitive material.
- Be sensitive to the clients' sense of pride and remember that they may experience some embarrassment regarding past experiences. Allow them to reflect on their own growth and be gentle about their past.
- Don't underestimate the value of the group process. Attending to the group process can help foster healthy attachments between group members. When facilitators are authentic, it can aid in the development of good connections.

7

CULTIVATING SELF-AWARENESS

Helping Clients Make Meaning from Experiences

Reflection: Why does self-awareness matter? As a therapist/facilitator, what steps can you take to actively work toward developing the self-awareness of your clients? How does your own self-awareness fit into being able to do this work?

Over half the expert facilitators with whom I spoke stressed the importance of promoting self-awareness within group clients by encouraging them to make meaning of their voices, visions, and unusual beliefs. When I was hospitalized for hearing voices and seeing visions, my mental health providers (although well-meaning) seemed committed only to making the voices and visions go away. They did not seem at all interested in providing me with psychoeducation/support groups/SOMETHING! to help me make sense of what was occurring in my mind.

Dazed and Confused with Voices

At the time of my hospitalization, I was scared, confused, missing my family and friends, and utterly at a loss as to what was happening in my mind. During the ten days I was in a psychiatric unit, the main focus was on stabilizing me with antipsychotic medications, and I had minimal contact with therapists or support staff. All of my fellow clients were very friendly, engaged me in lots of interesting conversations, and one young man (generously) exposed himself to me while I asked staff a question. The crew of clients on my unit were not verbally or physically aggressive, and were generally cooperative with staff. We definitely would have been able to handle participating in some form of group therapy. We clients only saw a group therapist one time during my stay in the acute unit. My individual therapist spoke with me twice—once upon admission, in which she asked about my symptoms, and again on the day I was discharged. What really surprised me was that amongst the clients—during meals or during cigarette breaks—people admitted to having extreme state experiences in hushed tones and with embarrassed expressions. Suicide attempts, homicidal thoughts, and sexual abuse all were openly discussed amongst clients during our time on the unit, but the grand taboo topic was hallucinations!

The mental health technicians during my stay clustered in the unit's office looking like bored babysitters. I craved conversation with people other than fellow clients, who were as perplexed about their voices and visions (if or when they chose to talk about them) as I was about mine. In all that time throughout the long and very boring days, I would have loved a group on how to cope with psychosis symptoms, someone to provide me with psychoeducation about voice hearing, or at the very least information regarding support groups such as Hearing Voices Network. None of this occurred, and the experience reinforced my embarrassment about hearing voices. Instead, a well-meaning therapist handed me a journal and said, "Put all your thoughts in this." She never came back to discuss what I wrote or to ask me questions about my voices or visions. I saw her one last time on the day before my discharge, when she provided a discharge interview. While I appreciated this therapist's attempt at helping me to cultivate self-awareness, her efforts felt lacking.

Trauma, Voices, and Self-Awareness

As discussed in the previous chapter, mental health researchers, and nearly all the mental health professionals with whom I spoke, believe that earlier trauma often serves as a trigger for extreme state experiences such as voice hearing. Over the years, I have found that clients in my voices and visions group unanimously have histories of trauma and/or abuse. Trauma certainly was one of the main triggers for my own voice hearing experiences. Unfortunately, research on trauma's impact on brain functioning suggests self-awareness goes "offline" during times of prolonged fear (Arnsten, Raskind, Taylor, & Connor, 2015; Bluhm et al., 2009). Researchers discovered when non-traumatized people are not thinking about anything, their natural resting state is self-reflection, based upon the areas of the brain which become activated (Bluhm et al., 2009). Folks with trauma do not do this, as observed by the lack of activity in the same area, which Dr. Bessel Van der Kolk (2014) refers to as "the mohawk of self-awareness" (e.g., orbital prefrontal cortex, medial prefrontal cortex, anterior cingulate, posterior cingulate, and insula). The traumatized brain does this as a form of self-protection—to shut down from over-arousal from external scariness. If a person is put into fear-inducing situations repeatedly and/or at critical periods in their life, their brain's ability to sense emotions may become shut down. A person's ability to sense their bodily sensations beyond their position in space goes offline, which could lead to an inability to feel like a self.

Consequently, this lack of a coherent sense of self leaves trauma survivors wide open to believing the criticisms and harmful narratives of their abusers, which I frequently see with my clients. Folks who grow up around abusive family members or abusers of one stripe or another may struggle to cultivate an authentic core self. Instead, they develop a pseudo-self, informed by the nasty messages, likes, and dislikes of those around them (e.g., "You suck!," "Worthless loser!," "Lazy Bastard!"). For folks who are predisposed to extreme state experiences, they may be holding up the mask of pseudo-self, AND underneath said mask may be harboring a vast collection of voices and visions, who are ALSO telling the person how to act and think! Clients I have worked with on inpatient units and crisis units often tell me of their struggles to distinguish the voices' beliefs from their own. This is hard to do when your internal sense of self is like a weak plant being choked out by the strong and weedy tendrils of nasty messages from past abusers and voices.

Why Self-Awareness Should Be Cultivated in a Group Setting

Here's the other thing to consider—voice hearers and others with extreme state experiences generally do not want to shake hands and make nice with their voices. Dr. Mark Hayward (2004) explored how people who have voices engage with their predominant voices from a position of distance, meaning "the voice hearers [are] suspicious and uncommunicative towards the voice that they were attempting to keep at a safe distance" (p. 377). Additionally, Hayward (2004, p. 380) points out the growing body of evidence, which suggests:

> *The ways in which voices are related to [by voice hearers] may reflect patterns of relating within the hearer's social world. Therefore, the way an individual relates to his or her voices may be influenced by past and present experiences of social contact.*

Although individual therapy is useful for voice hearers because they can explore the meaning of their voices or visions in a safe and private environment, hearing voices groups offer a different way of fostering self-awareness by helping clients develop a deeper understanding of their voices and visions with feedback from others who can relate. Past experiences of social relating can be challenged, discussed, and altered. Nearly all the expert facilitators with whom I spoke stated that a positive group outcome is when clients are able to understand how their voices, visions, and unusual beliefs fit into the narrative of their lives, and/or clients connect to the emotions related to these experiences. Below is an example of social relating, breaking old patterns, and voice hearing that occurred in my voices and visions group.

Case Example: Sally and Maude

I had two women in their sixties in my hearing voices group who lived in a group home together. Both women had intellectual disabilities in addition to diagnoses of schizoaffective disorder.

Maude often heard animal noises, which she found frightening and distracting. Sally, who lived down the hall, would see Maude walking down the hall and invite her to watch a DVD or visit together. Maude, according to Sally, would ignore these invitations, and Sally began to view Maude as a fair-weather friend. However, one day during group, Maude explained, "I'm not ignoring you, Sally. I'm hearing the animal noises, and they scare me." Sally quickly realized the misunderstanding, "Oh I thought you were ignoring me! But you were actually really scared. That's ok—just tell me. I hear scary things too. You can come into my room anytime and we can talk about it!" Maude reassured Sally, "I don't dislike you at all! You're my friend! I didn't mean to ignore you." Sally and Maude lived together for years in the same group home, both attended the same voices group, but never openly talked about how their voices impacted their social relating with one another—until that group.

Ways to Cultivate Self-Awareness for Voice Hearers

How can self-awareness be cultivated for folks whose core sense of self is uncertain or underdeveloped? Well, like when you grow plants in a garden, create a work of art, or build a house, a cleared space needs to be established. Aside from creating a holding space of emotional safety (see previous chapter), clients have taught me about the benefits of creating a mental holding space in their own minds. I did this exact thing while hospitalized so my voices and visions would feel less overwhelming. In my mind's eye, I would imagine a door being shut and locked, with the sign "Out to Live; Be Back Soon!" placed on the door. Over time, this technique allowed me to begin successfully developing control over my voices and visions. When I share this technique and its origin story with group clients, they begin discussing their own versions of "closed" or "be back soon" signs. One of my clients recently asked me to draw an "out to live" sign on the board for her, so she could commit the image to memory.

One expert facilitator I interviewed believes group members learn from one another via observing other group members as they reflect upon their psychosis-related symptoms. This encourages observing group clients to explore the meaning of their own psychosis-related experiences:

> *When we are suffering from psychosis … we don't have the ability on a regular basis to reflect, but if patients were to find themselves in the group and outside of the group to be able to think about their experiences, contemplate them … I think that groups in particular are very helpful in that other patients contribute in the sense that other patients over time take the position of the third … They're there to observe and experience what someone else is working on … [and] maybe they can do it for themselves.*

In the voices group I facilitate, observation is one of the most powerful tools, and clients often say how much they learn about themselves through listening to other group members.

Another of the expert facilitators, who identifies as an individual with lived experience with voices and visions, explained she encourages her group therapy clients to explore the meaning related to their voices, visions, and unusual beliefs:

> *People are having real experiences. They are actually hearing that voice or they're having those fears. Then communicating that it's a very meaningful experience even though it may need to be decoded. That's the heart of it.*

The experience of having other group members and the facilitator listen to one's experiences and not appear scared or condescending (more on this point later) is very validating for my clients. Often clients have told me (and I found this to be true in my own life) that they hold back what they say to others about their experiences. Imagine having this whole internal life and relationships with ones' voices but being unable to fully share them with loved ones. It felt (for me) like walking around holding a mental beach ball underwater while at the same time trying to appear undistracted and "normal." Think about this—how much mental energy would you exert if a large part of your social life (such as family relationships, friendships, romantic partners) could NEVER be discussed with ANYONE for fear of being considered "crazy" or worse—being hospitalized for having these "relationships." To put it simply—it sucked.

Case Example: Annie

In my group, clients often attend after being discharged from our clinic's crisis stabilization unit or a psychiatric inpatient unit. Several years ago, a 50-something-year-old female client, Annie, showed up in group and explained that she had just completed a ten-day stay on our crisis unit. She reported hearing muffled voices saying they were planning to poison her cat, and she was convinced someone was going to break into her home at any moment. Annie told the group she nailed her windows and doors shut to deter intruders from breaking into her home. After hearing Annie share her story, several long-term group members shared their own experiences managing their voices through boundary setting. Annie began crying as she listened to these group members speak. During a natural stopping point, one of the group members (a grandmotherly type with a strong southern accent) asked, "Annie, honey, why you cryin'? Is it something we said?" Another group member passed her tissues, and still another group member asked if she wanted a hug (she did). Annie explained, "You all function so well! And I never knew you could set boundaries with your voices! I am so afraid of mine, so I never thought to explore them!" Two years later, Annie no longer nails her windows and doors shut, is better able to manage her "paranoia" through boundary setting, and is hoping to one day become a mental health professional to help others.

The power of this particular experience was in watching group members share their own experiences, and Annie witnessed qualities (e.g., assertiveness, boundary setting, humor, compassion) in others she hoped to one day emulate. We can't be what we can't see! Groups for voice hearers allow people new to recovery to realize that there is hope, and to show them what healing can look like.

Processing the Process

Another expert facilitator also mentioned the importance of encouraging self-reflection within this client population and stated that he fosters this process through reflecting upon what was shared during the course of the group:

> *When there is a particularly challenging session … I will ask the process question at the end, "What was it like to talk about this stuff for the first time today?" What is interesting is getting them to reflect, so using that observing ego about something that just happened. I just know that if they don't learn to observe the process of therapy, how are they going to learn to observe themselves when times get tough? … [Teaching clients to] incorporate the kind of self-monitoring skills they might need when they don't have you is really important.*

I often ask long-term group members to share their experiences with newer or first-time group members. One of my long-term clients, Jeff, a 50-something white male with a strong Brooklyn accent (denoting his NYC roots), always drawls, "I feel like my thinking isn't so twisted! I'm not the only one who hears and sees things that aren't there." Other clients express appreciation for being allowed to discuss their experiences in detail, reflect on their voices without feeling judged, problem-solve ways to cope, or vent how some voices/visions are exacerbating their mood.

Another client, Jenna, a 30-something-year-old white female, was blown away when she first began attending the voices and visions group. As she sat through her first group, Jenna's initial stoic expression turned to shock and amazement while listening to long-term group members discuss their experiences. When I gently asked Jenna about her reactions to the other group members' stories, she burst out, "I am overwhelmed right now. I was expecting to be given a list of coping skills or told my voices were 'all in my head.' But instead, you guys talk about these experiences like they're real! I've always believed I was psychic but always just told doctors, 'Yes, I have hallucinations.' I didn't want to be in the hospitals longer than necessary. I'd lie and say my voices were gone when they really weren't. I've just got to sit here and think about what's being said." Jenna became a regular group member. Over time, she learned to set boundaries for her voices, figured out what triggered certain voices, began reading about psychic development, and increased her overall self-awareness regarding the origins of her extreme state experiences.

Naming the Voices

Over the years, many folks who attend my group give names to their voices, like "Bob," "The Mean Old Lady," "The Greek Chorus," or "Smitty." Group members will give periodic updates about their voices to one another, and often matter-of-factly inquire about one another's voices.

> *"Have you spoken with 'The Purple Clown' within the past few days?"*
> *"Have you seen 'Smitty' lately, and has he been bugging you at night?"*
> *"How did 'The Twins' react when you had that fight with your husband?"*

Clients intuitively know to ask about each other's voices or visions as real entities that others cannot see or hear. Since I run a group in Appalachia, this culture prides itself on being social and asking after others' loved ones in great detail. Therefore, I do not know how well this approach of asking after one's voices in such an extensive manner will translate into various cultures and other parts of the world. I suggest you play it by ear and see what works for your group.

Triggers for the Voices

An important area of increased self-awareness for my group clients are the triggers that exacerbate their extreme state experiences. Although some group members enjoy and welcome their voices/visions (such as my clients who identify as "psychic," "prophets," or "intuitive"), there are many group members who really dislike their voices and want them to go away! Several facilitators with whom I spoke stated that they encourage the development of client self-awareness through minimal interpretation of their clients' extreme state experiences. Instead, they focus on the emotional content. When asked why focusing on emotional content was helpful for clients within this population, one facilitator explained:

> *I would say in the majority of cases ... We were helping them express their emotional content because a lot of them weren't ready for the insight into it ... [because] their thought processes are disorganized.*

Again, this supports the discussion earlier in this chapter about trauma, the brain, and self-awareness. Helping group members identify their feelings and name those feelings is a huge deal, particularly for those folks who are alexithymic. I learned a memorable lesson about emotional process versus content during my very first counseling practicum at an inpatient behavioral psychiatric unit.

Case Example: Jay

I was in my second week as a counseling practicum student on an inpatient psychiatric unit, and my supervisor asked me to invite clients into the afternoon art therapy group. I approached one of the clients, a 30-something Latino male, Jay, and encouraged him to join the art therapy group down the hall. Although I knew some of his backstory—he recently witnessed the death of his friend, Michael, in a bar fight—I had never spoken with him directly. Jay walked toward me and asked to have a quiet word before entering the group room. "Can I speak with you, Miss? I want to make sure Michael is coming to group too. Have you seen him? I don't want to go to group without him."

I was stunned and knew he was speaking of his friend who had recently passed away. After a brief pause, I replied, "I am unsure where Michael is at the moment, but maybe he'll find his way to group." This answer seemed to satisfy Jay, and he followed me into the group room. Michael was never mentioned again during this group.

I later asked my supervisor, a very wise and patient counselor, Ms. Joyce, how to better respond to client comments and questions which do not seem grounded in my reality. (I purposely say "my reality" because I do not want to discredit the experiences or realities of others. In that moment with Jay, he truly believed his buddy was nearby and able to attend art therapy group. THAT was Jay's reality.) Ms. Joyce suggested addressing the emotional aspect of Jay's question. Instead of responding "as if" Michael was just around the corner, I could address Jay's question by replying, "It sounds like Michael is important to you, but right now you're here to focus on you. Let's go to group, and can we talk about Michael later?" I cannot guarantee this response will always work, but I will say (in my experience), addressing the emotional aspect of a voice, vision, or extreme state experience tends to be well-received by clients.

Therapist Self-Awareness

Several of the facilitators with whom I spoke stressed the importance of facilitators developing their own self-monitoring skills so as not to inadvertently harm or hinder their clients. One group facilitator explained his reasoning:

> *I think you need to be self-aware. It is important for any therapist, but especially important in working with this population, because it is so easy to get drawn into their undercurrent of psychosis, and the emotional undercurrent of affect, that you can get sucked right into if you don't have a good sense of who you are and what your stuff is.*

Before facilitating a hearing voices group, explore what your own thoughts are about working with this population. Asking the following questions of yourself might be helpful prior to taking on the awesome and (sometimes) wild task of running a voices group:

- Why do I want to run a hearing voices group?
- Do I have loved ones who experienced voices/visions, and what is/was my relationship with this person? How might these experiences impact my ability to do this work?
- Am I able to remain patient and process-oriented since progress often moves slowly with group members?
- Am I at ease and comfortable working with folks who hear voices or have visions? Why or why not?
- Is there another professional with whom I can co-facilitate, or regularly consult or receive supervision about running voices groups?
- How comfortable am I with clients who may not want to sit in the group circle, not speak for weeks at a time, or exhibit unusual behaviors (e.g., pacing, tardive dyskinesia-related movements, appear internally stimulated)?

Asking these questions of yourself is a useful way of gauging your level of readiness to facilitate a hearing voices group. Beyond examining your level of willingness and training, I would also encourage you to receive live clinical supervision regarding how to facilitate these groups. If you are lucky enough to observe a Hearing Voices group being run (and the group is willing to let you sit in), fantastic! Otherwise, seek out training!!! The Hearing Voices Network has group facilitator trainings throughout the country. Also, co-facilitate groups with an experienced clinician so she or he can help you improve as a group leader. As a supervisor, I am able to point out my supervisees' blind spots, strengths, and areas for growth. One of my own blind spots (which, thanks be to many supervisors—you know who you are!) that I have learned to develop awareness around was my tone of voice and reactions when speaking with clients.

How Does that Make You Feel? ... and Other Comments that Irritate Clients

Speaking to any clients (but particularly those who have voices and/or visions) in an authentic and NON-CONDESCENDING manner is incredibly important if you want to build any sort of rapport with them. Overhearing facilitators (or mental health clinicians in general) talk down to clients is a huge pet peeve of mine, both as a clinician and when I was a client. When I was hearing voices and asked to share my experiences with mental health professionals, I was hyper-aware of their non-verbal responses to how I answered their questions. Yes, I knew my experiences would not be believed! Of course, I anticipated their disbelief regarding my experiences, so I watched their faces for the slightest flicker of scorn or mocking judgment.

In 2015, I attended the International Society for Psychological and Social Approaches to Psychosis (ISPS) international conference in NYC and watched in awe as the voice hearers attending were treated with reverence by many (if not most) of the other attendees. Mental health clinicians from all over the world (some from fancy Ivy League universities!) were discussing the importance of treating voice hearers or "experts by experiences" as knowledgeable allies in treating psychosis-related disorders. I closely watched how these professors, psychiatrists, social workers, psychologists, and others responded to the voice hearers as they shared their personal experiences. Instead of disdainful looks, judgy quirked eyebrows, or overly politically-correct tiptoeing around symptoms, these mental health professionals looked on with matter-of-fact patience and curiosity. When they asked the voice hearers questions, they did not pitch their voices in that condescending way adults too often speak to a dim-witted pet or an overtired toddler. They posed questions in a calm and curious manner. I thought at the time, "If only I had been treated in this manner when I was hospitalized! I would have WANTED to share my story with the clinicians." I began training myself to emulate those therapists and clinicians I met at the ISPS conference through the use of live supervision, watching videos of myself provide services (client permission was always obtained beforehand), and my own self-awareness to better develop the ability to talk with clients in a matter-of-fact tone. Not going to lie—adjusting how I was in the room with clients was tough going at first.

Focusing on process over content can also be useful for group facilitators. Otherwise, one can get caught up in untangling the threads of a client's story, attempting to use detective work to make sense of the various details, or feeling pulled to jump in with advice to rescue a client from a perceived bad situation. As a means of illustrating my point, let me share a story about a client I encountered, Beth, a 50-year-old African American woman who intermittently attended one of my hearing voices groups.

Case Example: Beth

Beth attended my hearing voices group to better understand her past voice hearing experiences and to better learn how to cope with these experiences. Beth stated she heard her neighbors threatening to kill her through the walls of her apartment building. Group members expressed alarm and encouraged Beth to call the police. However, Beth indicated she had 45 cats in her apartment and did not want to get evicted for having so many pets. She later reported moving to another apartment (with only 25 cats), but again insisted her landlord, who lived upstairs, was threatening to kill her. Again, Beth refused to call the police, but stated she carried a switchblade on herself for protection. She abruptly stopped attending group, and fellow group members expressed concerns for Beth's safety. No one, including her individual therapist, knew what happened to her. But a little over a year later, she returned to group. Beth and her (now 65) cats were living in a trailer with her cousin, and the trailer was registered as a "cat sanctuary." Once more, she was concerned about her safety, and reported her cousin was threatening to kill her.

The clients in the hearing voices group, at that point, were unfamiliar with Beth, her cats, and the past roommate issues. They launched into giving her advice about moving, taking care of the cats (many of the group members were cat owners), and encouraged her to file a protection order against the cousin. Although I was not certain Beth was lying about her story, there certainly seemed to be a theme of threatened safety, concern for her animals, and helplessness. Instead of (a) calling the truth of Beth's stories into question, (b) trying to give advice about cat care and moving, or (c) sitting passively while the clients gave feedback, I did not get caught up in the content of Beth's stories. Instead, I focused on the process: themes of hopelessness, safety, feeling victimized, anger, and self-empowerment. I observed, "Beth, you have shared similar stories about threatening neighbors or landlords, correct?" (She agreed.) I went on to say, "In the previous two instances, you were able to leave these crappy situations with your cats, right?" (Again, she agreed.) Then I asked, "Tell me about how you were able to leave? Because it sounds like you were able to leave before, so you'll be able to leave again, right? Sometimes the voices tell us we're weaker, less reliable, less capable than we really are. I'm just reminding you that you left awful situations TWICE! You can figure out how to leave again." Beth didn't need a detailed outline about how to fix her life, but a reminder of her own efficacy to make necessary changes.

Addressing process over content helps clients develop their own self-awareness, allows them to see the patterns in their behavior, and (ideally) corrects unhealthy patterns of behavior. Furthermore, confusion and "twisted thinking" (as my client, Ben, puts it) go along with voices, visions, and unusual beliefs. Keeping the focus of the group dialogue primarily on "process thinking" (as my client, Stephen, calls it) models clear thinking and problem-solving methods, which increases self-awareness.

Summary Points

- There are opportunities, even during acute hospitalizations, to promote self-awareness and help patients make sense of their experiences, to cope with symptoms of psychosis, and to engage in psychoeducation and support groups.

- An overwhelming number of people who experience voices and visions have a history of trauma. This trauma appears to impact the brain and reduce the brain's ability to engage in self-awareness and contribute to a lack of a coherent sense of self.
- Positive group outcomes are when clients gain an understanding of how their voices, visions, and unusual beliefs fit into the narrative of their lives, and/or clients can connect healthy emotions to these experiences.
- Creating a mental holding space in the mind can help clients cultivate a sense of self-awareness. As clients develop greater self-awareness, they can understand triggers and begin to set boundaries with the voices and visions.
- Some clients benefit from focusing on the emotional content of extreme state experiences, rather than interpretations or insight.
- Before beginning to facilitate a hearing voices group, take the opportunity to explore your own thoughts and feelings about working with this population. Be sure you have another professional with whom you can consult, and be sure you develop a good sense of your own self-awareness.
- Within a group, focusing on the process over the content can be extremely useful for facilitators and can help clients continue to cultivate their own self-awareness.

References

Arnsten, A. F., Raskind, M. A., & Connor, D. F. (2015). The effects of stress exposure on prefrontal cortex: Translating basic research into successful treatments for post traumatic stress disorder. *Neurobiology of Stress, 1*(1), 89–99.

Bluhm, R. L., Williamson, P. C., Osuch, E. A., Frewen, P. A., Stevens, T. K., Boksman, K., Neufeld, R. W., Theberge, J., & Lanius, R. A. (2009). Alterations in default network connectivity in post traumatic stress disorder related to early-life trauma. *Journal of Psychiatry and Neuroscience, 34*(3), 187–194.

Hayward, M. (2004). Interpersonal relating and voice hearing: To what extent does relating to the voice reflect social relating? (2004). *Psychology and Psychotherapy Theory Research and Practice, 76*(4), 369–383.

Van der Kolk, B. (2014). *The body keeps the score. Brain, mind, and body in the healing of Trauma.* New York: Penguin Books.

8

ENCOURAGING EMPOWERMENT AMONG GROUP MEMBERS

Gaining a Sense of Control

> *Reflection: Do you believe voice hearers can develop control over their voices? Why or why not?*

When I talk with clients in my hearing voices groups, one of the recurrent themes they discuss is the lack of control they have over their voices and visions. When first experiencing my own voices, I struggled with wrangling them to not pop out at inopportune times. Mid conversation with a friend or family member, one of my voices would (loudly) crack a joke about that person's appearance or what they just said. I had such a hard time not cracking up, smiling, or responding to the voice because some of those jokes were pretty damn funny. When I was hearing voices, I felt at the mercy of their whims, demands, and needs. Like a chunk of human tofu, I began to absorb the flavors of my various voices—their thoughts and feelings, which at the time seemed wildly different than my "Andrea thoughts." My own need for independence from my voices—a separate thinking space—versus the voices' need for togetherness was a constant source of anxiety for me. I wish someone (a therapist, psychiatrist, mental health technician) would have told me, "YOU are in control of when the voices speak and don't speak! Your voices don't have to run your life."

Lost in the Crowd (in Our Minds)

Clients in my groups describe their voice hearing experiences in many ways: kind, bossy, mean, silly, threatening, nurturing, demanding, goofy, opinionated. Sam, a 52-year-old Caucasian male, expressed frustration with his voices because they frequently made negative comments about his appearance, behavior, and/or the sound of his voice.

Another group client, Amber, a 25-year-old African American female, said her voices were very menacing and threatening. "They kept saying they were going to hurt my dog, so I nailed all the windows and doors in my home shut." How scary and inconvenient! Each time Amber wanted to leave her house, she bent the nails back from the door frame to open her doors.

For many clients and myself, the voices are like a whole set of family and friends who comment on our lives, but these "individuals" all live in our heads. If these voices were being generated from "real live" people, a therapist or friend or family member might encourage the voice hearer to develop healthy boundaries, reframe how they think about these individuals, and/or learn to communicate with them in a healthier manner. How do we help clients to manage voices in their minds? There is no walking away, hanging up the phone, or shutting the door on a voice. (Plus, they often do not like being ignored!)

Crowd Control—Why Is Empowerment Important for Voice Hearers?

According to the facilitators whom I interviewed (and my own lived experience as a voice hearer and hearing voices group facilitator), fostering empowerment and healthier relationships between people and their voices is possible when working with clients who want increased control over their voices.

One of the facilitators with whom I spoke explained why fostering empowerment among clients who hear voices is important, and how group therapy can encourage this process:

> *I think it's very important to empower people who have these types of experiences, because they don't get empowered very often. I think a lot of times in society, they've [been told] "you're crazy" or "what you're saying doesn't make a lot of sense." So I think it is very important*

> *to have spaces for people to be empowered and feel in control of their own situation instead of rather than chemicals gone awry.*

My clients find inspiration in witnessing how other voice hearers in the group manage their experiences and manage the "crowd" in their minds. I once led a group where one of the newer group members burst into tears when fellow clients began talking about setting boundaries with their voices. When I inquired about the client's emotional reaction, he said, "I never imagined I could set boundaries with my voices! I never even considered this to be an option! I hope I can do this too." (Spoiler alert: He did! This client learned to empower himself, not allow the voices to control his life, and his quality of life drastically increased.)

Group Structure and Rules

How can facilitators who run voices groups foster this process among group members? Half the group leaders interviewed suggested clients be allowed to make decisions regarding how the group is structured (e.g., group rules, set up of the room). Many of the clients who attend my groups have long histories of inpatient hospitalizations, incarceration, and/or come from home environments where they felt trapped/held against their will. Rules were often forced upon them and they had no say in how their environment was structured.

Therefore, during the initial sessions of a voices group (e.g., when the group is initially started), I encourage clients to identify group rules and ask them how we as a group can enforce these rules. Periodically, I will hold a "state of the union" discussion regarding group rules and structure so newer clients can share their opinions, and the "old guard" clients can make suggestions as well. These sessions appear to be well-received based upon clients' level of participation, feedback, and enthusiasm. The topics we cover in these talks include but are not limited to:

- How late group members can arrive.
- Cell phone usage during group.

- Eating/drinking during group.
- When and how to provide feedback to fellow group members.
- How to react when someone's belief system is different from your own.
- Relationships between clients outside of the group room.
- How to cope if one feels overwhelmed or experiences a panic attack during group.

These group discussions have led to wonderful suggestions by clients, increased group bonding, and fantastic discussions regarding healthy communication skills. Throughout my years as a group leader, I have seen clients frequently react with thinly veiled hostility and/or resentment when group rules are forced upon them. If facilitators want to propose a new group rule, including clients in the development process is (in my experience) better received by group members, and this is particularly true with this client population.

Sit Where You Want

Several facilitators suggested clients be allowed to sit where they want in the group room—even if this means they sit outside the "group circle." One facilitator explained the importance of allowing flexibility in seating this way:

> *It's … about agency … Any way you can make people feel empowered will help them as well[,] such as not make them sit in the circle. Anything to encourage [clients] to have agency by allowing them to sit however they want in this room.*

Clients in my group typically sit in a circle, but newer clients have been known to sit outside the circle. Although I encourage them to join in the rest of the group, I do not force the issue if they decline.

Coping Skills for Voice Hearers

How often have you discussed coping skills with your clients? Hundreds of times? Thousands? Why are coping skills so important for voice hearers, and why are group discussions about them so necessary? Over half the facilitators that were interviewed mentioned the importance of teaching active coping skills to help clients better manage their more frustrating/intrusive voices and/or the difficult emotions connected to these experiences. One facilitator commented on how coping skills can help increase emotional self-regulation:

> *You would want access to some … kind of active coping … if they needed time out from group. Or [if] they were emotionally overloaded, they could go over to that table and sit with themselves, recollect, and rejoin the group … You're fostering agency. You're fostering [the clients'] own ability to control their emotional regulation, [because this client population] have a hard time controlling their emotions, so they hallucinate.*

Ian, a 29-year-old male who often heard command hallucinations to harm others, says his coping skills keep him grounded. Over our year of working together, he expanded his coping skills from smoking pot and playing first-person shooter video games to cooking, reading, playing with his fidget spinner toy, (still lots of) video gaming, and drawing. Ian stopped the pot smoking on his own after realizing (in our individual sessions and in group sessions) that this "coping skill" exacerbated his voices.

When I run groups on coping skills, clients are very enthusiastic participants, and great discussions occur between members regarding what works for them. Below are some of the client-generated coping skills.

Listening to Music

Make sure the music does not promote/encourage exacerbation of voices. Different music works for different folks—some clients like country, others heavy metal, and still others love classical. However, most clients do agree music that promotes violence is never very helpful.

Spiritual Practices

I cover this topic in more detail below; however, clients often find a spiritual practice (e.g., attending church, carrying crystals, attending Bible study, smudging) helps them cope with their voices, or with the anxiety which arises from hearing voices.

Exercise

I work in a community mental health center, and my clients' financial resources to pay for gym memberships are limited. However, taking walks in the local park, around the neighborhood, or even around the apartment building is a free and popular way clients can distract themselves from voices.

Carry a Cell Phone or Realistic Toy Phone

If the voices are screaming at you, yelling back at them in public is often frowned upon by those who are nearby. A client in one of my groups once said, "I carry a cell phone (it has no minutes on it, but still) so I can pretend to be on it and yell back at the voices. That way no one thinks I'm nuts!" So ingenious! When voices strike, the urge to respond is unbearable—I know. This coping skill is very popular with group members.

Engage in Hobbies

Finding an activity to distract from the voices is a popular way clients cope. Cooking, video gaming, playing cards, drawing/painting, gardening, fishing, and four-wheeling (you can tell I work in a rural area) are some of the hobbies my clients have reported using to cope with their voices. (My group members recently taught me to play poker during a group about coping skills and were excellent poker coaches! They had a blast showing me and others how to play. Plus, they enjoyed teaching me something—for a change!) Reading can be challenging for some folks, because the voices may distract from the story and lead to frustration.

Managing Stress Levels

This is imperative, as many clients agree increased levels of anxiety, anger, stress, or depression inevitably lead to increases in their voice hearing. Clients learn to recognize that their stress levels are too high when voices emerge or increase, and they make lifestyle adjustments accordingly. These may include cutting back on work or school responsibilities, limiting being around people who stress them out, getting more sleep, or eating healthier—whatever works.

Eliminate or Cut Back on Drug or Alcohol Usage

Group clients frequently say they notice a correlation between substance use and their voices. When clients use street drugs (especially marijuana and hallucinogens) and/or alcohol, they notice their voices become more pronounced, nastier, and/or scarier. When these clients discontinue their substance use or cut way back, the voices recede.

Talk to Someone about These Experiences

Having a trusted friend, therapist, or family member to share your stories and struggles with is very helpful for all my clients (and for myself). When I was actively hearing voices, everyone I told (e.g., doctors, family) reacted in fear, confusion, or wrote out a prescription. I felt isolated, angry, confused, and embarrassed. All the more reason for a safe space like a hearing voices group, right?

Journaling

Whether you encourage clients to write or draw, sorting out the "yarn ball" of thoughts and emotions which rattle around their minds is helpful—especially if there are opinionated voices in their heads. I have many clients keep track of when they hear voices (e.g., time of day/day of the week), their emotional state, and what they are doing (e.g., are you alone, with friends/family, at work). The clients are then encouraged to share these entries in individual sessions or with the group. Tracking voices has helped many clients recognize their triggers and make lifestyle adjustments. (Also, never assume a client's intellectual abilities preclude them from keeping journals. Some of the most enthusiastic journalers I have in group or as individual clients have intellectual disabilities.)

Socialize

Pablo, a 55-year-old Latino male, discovered he only heard voices when alone or while watching television (which he did all day long). While attending group, this client realized he did not hear voices while socializing with friends or neighbors. This prompted my client to increase his socializing, and he went from a solitary existence to having a girlfriend and several buddies with whom he spends time. His voices still occur, but they are much less upsetting since he expanded his social circle.

Laughter

The clients in my group often joke about their voice hearing experiences with one another. Sure, they are respectfully serious and provide thoughtful feedback when the moment calls for it. However, they enjoy nothing more than laughing or cracking jokes about one another's voices or visions. This is the power of the group! Clients also report that listening to comedy podcasts or watching funny movies also helps keep their anxiety and sadness down, which in turns keeps voices at bay. Cheryl, a 45-year-old African American female, stated she saw fairies in her apartment and the whole experience freaked her out. "However, I wanted to be a good hostess, so I fed Tart n' Tinys candies to the fairies, because I am able to laugh at the situation." This led to a lively discussion by group members regarding the dietary habits of fairies, and if Mountain Dew was an acceptable fairy beverage.

Lived Experience

I encourage clients to seek out books, websites, podcasts, and/or YouTube videos created by individuals with lived experiences with voices. The Hearing Voices Network website (www.hearing-voices.org) also provides a wonderful list of coping skills and other resources which are very useful and generally well-received by the members of my group. Other websites such as Mad in America are awesome resources and are well-received by many clients. These are websites/organizations run by voice hearers for voice hearers. Clients have said they love the resources on this website and find the tips very helpful, practical, and effective. There are resources such as Eleanor Longden's TED Talk, "The Voices in My Head" (2013; a personal favorite), or Ron Coleman and Mike Smith's book, *Working with Voices: From Victim to Victor* (2006) (another fave). I also disclose some of my own experiences in brief vignettes. There are certain stories I share with clients if the moment is appropriate and serves the client's therapeutic process. (That is my own choice, and I would encourage facilitators to share only to the degree that they are comfortable. My general rule in self-disclosure is this—*share scars, not wounds.* If an emotional injury is still healing, you might want to hold back on sharing the story with others and particularly with clients.)

Voices, Medications, and Non-Western Medical Treatments

A word about medications—overall, I believe medications such as antipsychotics, mood stabilizers, antidepressants, and anxiolytics can be very helpful in assisting some people with managing their symptoms. I always tell my clients that taking medication is a personal decision they must make for themselves, and I never force clients into doing something that makes them uncomfortable. We explore what potential options might work best for them, and this approach is very well-received by clients in both individual and group therapy.

When I was hospitalized during my acute psychotic episode, I was prescribed a large number of medications that left me feeling lethargic, caused excessive drooling (not a cute look), and left me unable to read anything more taxing than the coupon section of the Sunday paper. This was a vast change from my previous level of functioning—a full-time doctoral student who held down a part-time job and routinely polished off an entire novel per week (on top of my school assignments). Thankfully, upon discharge, I was able to work with a very knowledgeable psychiatrist who gently adjusted my medications. Within six weeks after discharge I was back to myself. Eventually, and with my psychiatrist's blessing, I was titrated off the antipsychotic medication and have been free of voices for six years. The moral of the story: medications can be helpful, but listen to your clients when they say the meds are making them feel awful! My side effects were so bad I had anxiety about whether or not my mind would ever go back to normal. I can understand why people on antipsychotic medications would consider going off them. Be patient with your clients who take themselves off their medications or continuously return back to their prescribers for medication adjustments. Sometimes getting the right "cocktail" of meds takes time. This is why helping clients work on developing alternative coping skills is so essential. One of the expert facilitators that I interviewed explained that teaching clients to develop active coping skills may also help them be less reliant upon medications, which is very desirable for many clients with psychosis-related symptoms:

> *You can understand why people might not want to take the medication or, uh, even stigma attached with the medication … "I don't mind taking my high blood pressure medication, [but] you know the 'crazy pill' that's a different story" … But just to have a few coping skills in their bag of tricks. "I want to go to bed. Okay, how can I get myself ready for bed without the voices keeping me up half the night without necessarily having to resort to medication?"*

Some of my clients in group do not take antipsychotic medications and have no interest in taking them. Many of these clients believe their voices are spirits of people who passed away, spirit guides, or demons. In the case of many such clients, we discuss non-Western healing methods for managing these voices, such as burning sage, Reiki, carrying crystals, using essential oils, and meditations. These group discussions (at least with my clients) are always very lively, and the local community where we live has several metaphysical shops and knowledgeable herbalists. I know many of my clients have found relief from their negative voices and felt more empowered after saging their homes, taking herbal tinctures, and/or carrying particular crystals.

I do not discount the power of non-Western interventions or coping tools when working with this population. Different interventions work for everyone, and I am glad they find these interventions to be effective. When clients ask me, "Do you think I'm nuts for believing in this stuff (e.g., crystals, essential oils, Reiki)?" I tell them, "Nope! The world is a mysterious place! If *smudging, crystals, meditation, essential oils* works for you, go for it! Some folks believe in rosary beads and holy water. Others find power in prayer. Different things work for different people!" It is also an issue of cultural respect, because many of my clients identify as Pagan or Wiccan, so I would never want to discount or dismiss their religious or spiritual beliefs.

Building Healthier Relationships with Voices in Our Heads

According to several of the expert facilitators with whom I spoke, another way empowerment can be cultivated amongst group members is to encourage them to develop healthier relationships with their voices. Several studies that explored what clients view as good AVH group outcomes indicated they feel more empowered and able to cope because of their improved relationships with their voices (Goodliffe, Hayward, Brown, Turton, & Dannahy, 2010; Hendry, 2011; Newton, Larkin, Melhuish, & Wykes, 2007). One of the facilitators provided an example of how controlling and demanding voices can shift for some clients, and how group members can become empowered to take back control of their lives:

> *[One of my clients] had a pretty terrible voice that locked [him] in the closet ... [He] lived in fear, in terror of this voice ... but*

> *based upon [learning about] other people's experiences [within the group] and other people in the group's questions for [him], [the client] ended up feeling more in control of the situation. And accepting that [the voice] is here now. Sometimes [the voice] disappears now. When [the voice] is here, I don't need to follow everything he says.*

From my work with voice hearers and my own lived experiences, I began to theorize that our relationships with the voices are often a reflection of our relationships with others in our lives, such as friends, family, and colleagues. Hayward's (2003) study regarding relating to voices suggested there may be two ways of working to modify clients' relationships with voices. The first way is through improving self-esteem and social relating skills, such as through group therapy. The second way is through decreasing negative relating of the hearer to the voice and vice versa. There are many ways to do this, but below are some ways to initially empower clients in their interactions with their voices.

In my groups, I encourage clients to set healthy boundaries with their voices, as well as with other people in their lives. When clients set healthy boundaries with their voices, they often find their boundaries with family and friends improving, and vice versa. My group clients do this in several ways:

- Saying to their voices, "Right now I'm busy, but I would love to talk with you later today. I will speak with you at 7:30pm tonight!"
- Telling their voices, "I will only respond to you when you are respectful to me."
- Explaining to their voices (either in their minds or out loud) how they feel about the voice's ongoing critical comments. (This often is best done in the company of a trusted person such as their therapist, family member, or friend.)

Clients have stated "training" their voices is much like teaching a puppy or child to do something new. There may be yelling, fussing, peeing on the floor (just kidding), but with patience and consistency, the efforts pay off. Again, many voice hearers view their voices as people and/or loved ones. They do not want them to "just go away," or perhaps despite multiple medication attempts, the voices will not leave. Therefore, discussing the development of healthy relationships, communications, and boundary setting is a way to empower clients to better manage the voices in their minds. Developing self-awareness regarding one's voices is also very empowering, and is addressed in the previous chapter.

Advocating for Themselves

Finally, a couple of group facilitators with whom I spoke indicated that empowering clients in group often led members to respectfully and openly question the treatment decisions made by their doctors. They learned to do this in a thoughtful way, such as by asking questions about their medications, or by not viewing treatment team members "with blind adoration of parental figures." Clients in my group, I have learned, refrain from discussing their therapists in front of me (because they are often my colleagues), but will frequently discuss their opinions of their treatment team members during a cigarette break before or after group. They find these conversations helpful, normalizing, and cathartic because they often share opinions on various clinicians. These informal conversations would not necessarily occur if the client was at a clinic for individual therapy or a medication check appointment. The ideas, tips, and suggestions in this chapter are hopefully a jumping off point for more ways you can empower the clients in your hearing voices group. Keep in mind the importance of working to empower and cultivate agency in this client population.

Summary Points

- Often, clients have come from experiences (e.g., hospitalization, incarceration, family settings) in which they were disempowered or trapped, which is why empowerment can be an important aspect of recovery.

- Include clients in the development of group rules and regulations to cultivate agency.
- Allow clients the freedom to sit where they want and to come and go when they need to (so long as they are discreet and do not wildly disrupt the group flow).
- Discuss healthy coping skills with clients and how use of coping skills cultivates increased control over voices.
- Medication is a personal decision. Many clients "can't live without their meds," and some individuals find non-Western medical interventions more effective. Allowing an open discussion regarding both approaches can be helpful.
- Encourage clients to discuss and explore how they can develop healthier relationships with their voices. Not everyone wants their voices to go away, so do not assume this is the end game.

References

Coleman, R., & Smith, M. (2006). *Working with voices—Victim to victor* (2nd ed.). Lewis, Scotland: P&P Press.

Goodliffe, L., Hayward, M., Brown, D., Turton, W., & Dannahy, L. (2010). Group person-based cognitive therapy for distressing voices: Views from the hearers. *Psychotherapy Research, 20*(4), 447–461.

Hayward, M. (2003). Interpersonal relating and voice hearing: To what extent does relating to the voice reflect social relating? *Psychology and Psychotherapy Theory Research and Practice, 76*(4), 369–383.

Hendry, G. L. (2011). *What are the experiences of those attending a self-help hearing voices group: an interpretive phenomenological approach.* University of Leeds.

Longden, E. (2013). The voices in my head. [Video file]. Retrieved from https://www.ted.com/talks/eleanor_longden_the_voices_in_my_head.

Newton, E., Larkin, M., Melhuish, R., & Wykes, T. (2007). More than just a place to talk: Young people's experiences of group psychological therapy as an early intervention for auditory hallucinations. *Psychology & Psychotherapy: Theory, Research & Practice, 80*(1), 127–149.

9

LIVING PROOF

Integrating Lived Experience to Inspire Hope

> *Reflection: Do you believe recovery is possible from voice hearing? What does recovery mean to you? Not hearing the voices? Living with the voices?*

Are people who have voices and visions (which may impact their functioning) able to live fulfilling lives? This was not something I thought much about until experiencing my own psychiatric hospitalization for voice hearing. Upon being discharged from the psychiatric hospital, I was determined to return to school for fall semester of my doctoral program (in clinical psychology no less). Although I felt shaky (but voice free), I signed up for classes. My psychiatrist, the discharging staff at the psychiatric hospital, and my family all encouraged me to "go easy," and to enroll in the hospital's intensive outpatient program. I arrogantly believed, "Nah, I don't need that," because (if I must be honest with myself) I did not believe in the power of group therapy. But in one of many synchronistic occurrences that year, the mental health clinic where I was completing my psychology practicum had an intensive outpatient group, and I was assigned to shadow the group leader.

Observing the facilitator help clients work through difficult emotions and thoughts taught me about the value of group therapy. Regular attendees to group began reporting ongoing increases in functioning, decreased symptoms, and overall return of hope. Sitting in the group several days a week with the clients helped me better understand several of my own issues.

(This group stuff actually works, who'd have thought?) Additionally, as a co-facilitator, I became aware how no group member discussed their voices, visions, or other extreme state experiences. I knew several group clients had these experiences because they were my individual therapy clients at the clinic. Later, I mentioned my observations about clients' reluctance in sharing their psychosis-related symptoms in group to the Intensive Outpatient Program (IOP) director, who (in another twist of fate) said, "Oh, several of the therapists here are developing a specialized group just for voice hearing. Would you like to be part of the development process?" Yes, please!

Had I never experienced the shame of being amongst peers in the psychiatric hospital and not wanting to share my voice hearing experiences, I would NEVER have been sensitized to group clients' apparent reluctance in sharing their psychosis-related experiences with others. I would have assumed (naively) that clients either (a) did not have these experiences or (b) they did not find their extreme state experiences bothersome enough to share with the group. I am grateful for having lived experience, as it made me aware of the shame in experiencing voices and having no one with whom to share these experiences.

The agency's clinical director, a psychologist, a licensed clinical social worker, and I all spent several months outlining goals, objectives, and interventions for the clinic's new group for voice hearers. Although uncomfortable with openly sharing about my lived experience (yet) with co-workers at this agency, I used (my secret knowledge) enthusiasm and curiosity to guide my involvement with developing the group curriculum. We had difficulties finding guidelines to running such a group—practical considerations such as group goals, room set up, interventions, etc. The International Society for Psychological and Social Interventions for Psychosis (ISPS) and the Hearing Voices Network (HVN) were helpful resources. I learned of these organizations because—another bit of synchronicity—one of my psychology professors that fall, Dr. Lewis Mehl-Madrona, was actively involved with both organizations (e.g., spoke regularly at their conferences and workshops) and happened to mention these organizations to my class one day.

Reading the ISPS literature and exploring the HVN's resources fueled my sense of optimism that voice hearers could live meaningful lives and that their experiences were of value to researchers. And not in a test monkey, "try this pill," sort of way. Voice hearers are called "experts by experience" within the ISPS. They were group facilitators of Hearing Voices groups. I, who had never considered myself to be an expert on anything (save how to make a fantastic grilled cheese sandwich), could be considered an *EXPERT* on a topic that I was previously too ashamed to discuss with anyone in my life.

Throughout the development of the group curriculum, I refrained from "outing myself" as a former voice hearer because I was aware of the stigma even amongst other mental health professionals. My level of comfort with openly sharing my voice hearing history took several more years to develop. There were periods of time that were rough (2012, I'm talking to you), but I would never give up these experiences because they provided me opportunities to help fellow voice hearers. Being a hospitalized voice hearer, sitting in the IOP group, learning how to lead my own hearing voices groups, writing this book, and now serving as a clinical leader and supervisor at the mental health clinic where I presently work taught me about hope.

I look back on my own struggles with voices and realized why I was so reluctant to attend the outpatient therapy groups suggested by the hospital staff. My presenting concern, as they say, was "hearing voices," but I was not prepared to share my experiences in mixed company. How would the group facilitator see me? With pity? Fear? *No thank you.* That's why I believe bringing my story into the voices group I facilitate is powerful. While I don't tell all of the gory details, I share enough to underscore my main point: Recovery is possible. Learning how to manage your voices and visions is possible. Will it take hard work, courage, vulnerability, and fear? Yes. Conducting research about voice hearing, facilitating a group on hearing voices, talking with clients about their lived experiences, and eventually discussing my lived experience with a trusted therapist all helped me to work through my thoughts and feelings about my voice hearing. Meditation, yoga, and connecting with a higher power were also crucial to my ability to make sense of my lived experiences. Getting quiet, turning off the television, sitting in contemplation, and taking some time to understand what happened (even when family and friends wanted to spend time with me) was also part of my recovery.

I certainly cannot discuss the importance of bringing narrative of lived experience into the group room without discussing how I prepared myself to do so. As I completed my dissertation research on voice hearing (the seed of this book), I meditated and prayed A LOT about whether to openly share my own lived experience with my dissertation committee. It wasn't until I was nearly at the end of my dissertation process that I told them. Taking the time to practice openly sharing my story, even in a small way, felt like necessary practice in more openly sharing my story with colleagues. Thankfully, the colleagues I initially told were supportive, kind, and (most importantly) handled my share in a matter-of-fact manner. While working through my voice hearing experience and dismantling the shame my experience initially evoked, my sense of pride in what I accomplished increased (building a meaningful life, improved self-awareness, a strong sense of resilience), and I now share that sense of pride with each voices group I run. While still being aware of the memories of the emotions and experiences related to my voice hearing, the feelings of embarrassment and shame I used to feel when sharing this story have dissolved. Deciding to openly share my story of recovery wasn't easy, but it's been worth it. Hopefully my share will spark someone else's desire to open up, feel proud of the difficulties endured, and help another voice hearer believe they can recover too. THAT'S the power of sharing a story of lived experience.

The literature on clients' views regarding mechanisms of change for AVH groups explores and supports the concept of encouraging "recovery"-minded thinking and introducing recovery narratives into the group room (Dillon & Hornstein, 2013; Hendry, 2011; Jones, Marino, & Hansen, 2015; Newton, Larkin, Melhuish, & Wykes, 2007; Webb, 2011). Many of the facilitators I interviewed also stressed the importance of bringing in the narratives of people who have lived experience with psychosis and are in recovery into the group room to instill hope within the group members. One facilitator explained why doing so is a powerful intervention for this client population:

> *You know, the power of people that have recovered or reframed their experiences and are living … the lives that they want to live … To at least have the kind of hope, if they're starting from a place of hopelessness or being quite a victim of the system, you know having really low self-esteem … To have some exposure … that that's not all there is out there and move through those problems and identities that are different from those and that's not even to say you should do that? But it's possible to do that.*

A few of the facilitators shared that bringing recovery narratives into the group room also encourages clients to feel a sense of pride or belonging. As one of the facilitators stated:

> *Even if you're not a voice hearer, bringing their narrative into the room I've found to be immensely helpful for people, and just giving themselves a sense of pride and "Hey, I belong to this group of people, who are not necessarily ill or disturbed, [but are] like an excellent group of people."*

A Sense of Belonging

When I come into the room for my Wednesday Voices and Visions group, there is an air of conviviality amongst group members. Over the months, and in some cases years, they share their stories of voice hearing, their fears about being hospitalized once more, announce with shy pride, "I haven't heard any voices in several weeks," and bemoan nasty side effects of various medications (or the dismissive attitudes of their prescribers). Upon entering this space, I don't try to "lead" the conversation so much as "join in" the conversation. I'll insert myself into the ongoing discussions in the room and (try to) subtly gauge the emotional temperature of the room as I ask questions, exchange fist bumps, and make sure coffee has been made. This approach seems to work well with my group because it is such a contrast to how they are often "talked at" by well-meaning group leaders, family members, and mental health providers.

Training for Facilitators

Many of the facilitators I interviewed also stressed the importance of receiving training from facilitators who have lived experience and are in recovery, such as Hearing Voices Network-trained facilitators. One facilitator explained why receiving training from individuals who have recovered is empowering:

> *I think that the training that I had with the H[earing] V[oices] N[etwork] teachers, you know? What's like provided by Western Mass … The National Empowerment Center … Um, you know people, who are recovered, that that's essential of course. That they be part of the training. 'Cause people just don't believe [in recovery].*

The facilitators with whom I spoke did not all have HVN training, but all participated in the workshops, conferences, and trainings which support the use of lived experience-related narratives in both group and individual therapy work.

Two of the facilitators interviewed stated they have lived experience and are in recovery. Both mentioned how they utilized their unique perspective to work with their group clients:

> *I think … what impacts [clients] the most is probably talking about your own lived experience. I tend to think so because … It's like you've got these two white middle class older women up … in front of a group of … people with, you know, very different*

> *backgrounds from ours … so to bridge the gap[,] you know … you go, "Hey, we are really different from you in some ways but we share some of these experiences." I think that leads to more open sharing.*
>
> *I would say that my lived experience really helped me to interpret what people are telling me in ways that required some discernment or decoding … when I met people who had extreme states or spoke metaphorically, I was really comfortable hanging out with them and exploring it.*

I feel the same way—it does not even occur to me to feel uncomfortable or on edge in room full of voice hearers or folks with psychosis-related disorders. Sitting in the group room and discussing people's extreme state experiences is comfortable for me as well. Also, I bring my personality and "my heart" into the room (to quote one of the interviewees), which I believe contributes to the success of the voices group. I encourage the clients to sing, laugh, talk about our extreme state experiences, drink coffee, discuss spiritual matters, dance, cry, eat snacks—in other words, to embrace our humanity along with the parts of ourselves which have *isolated us from other humans* in the past.

The facilitators who encouraged others to receive training from individuals with lived experience had many recommendations regarding where and with whom to seek out such training. Several facilitators mentioned they received training through the Hearing Voices Network (HVN), which offers group facilitation workshops for this client population and is run by individuals with lived experience. Over half the facilitators stated they utilized HVN-related articles and resources in their groups for this client population.

If You Don't Have Lived Experience … Be Curious!

Many of the facilitators I spoke with did not have lived experience, but they did report a strong curiosity about voice hearing and other extreme state experiences. Having a person, especially a mental health professional like a therapist, nurse, or psychiatrist, express an authentic interest in one's voices is not always common. As one facilitator explained:

> *It's not that people don't mean to help … but it's not uncommon for someone to say, 'that's just a hallucination and it doesn't mean anything' … because they don't want to reinforce it … Sometimes people think if you're going to try to talk to people about this and you're going to try to understand it, that you're going to push people into actions that are harmful. And it does take some skill. You have to strike a balance.*

Another facilitator with whom I spoke discussed why curiosity is important when working with clients who hear voices:

> *I think you have to be curious. I think that the best therapist with this population are more curious than your average therapist. Because there's no one thing that causes this situation. You have to be open to what's going to land in your lap and be willing to tolerate that not knowing. It's true for clients, especially clients with psychosis, because people get to be this way from many different ways. You have to be able to tolerate with not knowing for long periods of time. If you can't, it's going to be hard.*

Through expressing curiosity and a genuine interest in clients' voice hearing experiences, facilitators encourage clients themselves to feel less afraid and avoidant of their voice hearing experiences:

> *I think one of the things that gets in the way is that people who have these experiences have been through a lot of medicalizing and pathologizing of their experience … Even though I don't have these experiences, I tend to be the least pathologizing person in the group … Getting people to look at their voices in a different way I think is hard, because there are some people that feel this is an illness. 'I have schizophrenia' and maybe that is helpful for that person.*

> *I'm not saying no one should feel that way ever. Maybe believing that helps them feel control, but if that is the predominant—"No, that is what it is!" and shuts down explanation. They don't get curious! They're like, I have this answer and even though I'm going to get a little curious, I still am going to end up back there at some point. It's so ingrained.*

Encouraging group members (together) to face thoughts, feelings, and VOICES they previously thought were scary monsters teaches them about their own capacity for bravery. Watching my group members return to group each week (with eagerness and smiles) is such a cool thing to experience as a facilitator. These amazing folks embody my favorite definition of bravery: being scared of what they have to share, but they do it anyway! (Gaiman, 2006). Cultivating one's bravery is never done in peace and comfort. It takes effort. Deciding to "out" myself as someone who has lived experience with voice hearing was not an easy decision. However, I would have felt like a hypocrite writing a book like this one without being open about my own lived experience. My group members have taught me about having pride in my lived experience, and I hope I have helped them feel some pride in their lived experiences too.

Summary Points

- It is difficult to self-disclose experiences of hearing voices and having visions, as the fear of stigma and uncertainty of how it will change one's perception is significant.
- Sharing a lived experience can help others feel more comfortable talking about their own experiences, and reduce their sense of being alone. It can also help others realize that recovery is possible and that there can be life beyond the voices and visions.
- Even if the facilitator is not a voice hearer, bringing in narratives of others who have lived experience with psychosis and are in recovery can help instill hope within the group members.

- Facilitators who do not have lived experiences with psychosis can be very effective if they indulge a strong curiosity about voice hearing and other extreme state experiences and have a genuine interest in clients' experiences.

References

Dillon, J., & Hornstein, G. A. (2013). Hearing voices peer support groups: A powerful alternative for people in distress. *Psychosis: Psychological, Social and Integrative Approaches*, *5*(3), 286–295.

Gaiman, N. (2006). *Coraline*. New York: HarperCollins Publishers.

Hendry, G. L. (2011). *What are the experiences of those attending a self-help hearing voices group: an interpretive phenomenological approach*. University of Leeds.

Jones, N., Marino, C., & Hansen, M. (2015). The hearing voices movement in United States: Findings from a national survey of group. *Psychosis*, *8*(2), 106–117.

Newton, E., Larkin, M., Melhuish, R., & Wykes, T. (2007). More than just a place to talk: Young people's experiences of group psychological therapy as an early intervention for auditory hallucinations. *Psychology & Psychotherapy: Theory, Research & Practice*, *80*(1), 127–149.

Webb, J. (2011). *Hearing voices: Coping, resilience and recovery*. University of Leeds.

10

CONCLUSIONS

Summary and Practical Tips

> *Reflection: Now that I know what I know, what steps can I take to apply this knowledge to working with people who hear voices, see visions, and/or have extreme state experiences? How can I be more effective as a facilitator?*

The facilitators with whom I spoke shared a wide range of ideas, commentary, and feelings about running groups for voice hearers. From these discussions, I distilled the six main themes: emotional safety, flexibility, group process, self-awareness, empowerment, and lived experience. I have come to embrace these principles in the facilitation of my own hearing voices group. Much to the surprise of my coworkers, the Voices and Visions group is consistently well-attended (between five to ten group members show up each week), discussions are very lively, and I am lucky enough to witness folks' daily functioning improving. Administrators, fellow therapists, and medical staff both seem intrigued and confused by the group. Typically I have conversations that follow this usual trajectory:

Coworker:	"You're running a group with a room full of voice hearers? Really?"
Me (unfazed):	"Yep! We have a good time and clients find it helpful."
Coworker:	"People actually ... show up? How many attend?"
Me:	"Yes. Between five to ten."
Coworker:	"What do you talk about?"

Me:	"Voices and visions ... and unusual beliefs." [thinking: "duh"]
Coworker:	"Wow." ... [speechless]

This interaction used to be fairly typical at the agency where I first started facilitating voices groups. However, now the group (in all its enthusiastic glory) is simply an accepted part of the culture where I work. A coworker whose office is near the group room told me, "I was doing therapy with a client and he heard singing and laughing coming out of the room during your group. He began looking confused and a little startled. I told him, 'Roll with it. Just the hearing voices group. Nothing to be alarmed about—typical for them.' He seemed to settle down after that."

Don't get me wrong, the group interactions aren't all rainbows and butterflies. Serious discussions about symptoms, trauma-related experiences, and the stigma of being a voice hearer are regular topics of discussion. As with any group, there are setbacks (people are hospitalized, clients stop attending and return with increased symptoms), and as a group leader, I embrace these struggles. No sense in trying to gloss over these experiences—I'm a naturally upbeat person but no Pollyanna. Group members and I talk about recent re-hospitalizations, the changes in medications, the mixed feelings of eagerness and fear of being discharged from a psychiatric hospital stay. However, I also see the improvements in my clients: watching previously emotionally shut down "Carl" dance his way around the group room like Mick Jagger in a music video, seeing shy "Katie's" face light up when she sees regular group members enter the room and listening to her crow, "Hi, Amber! Hi Ethan!! How are you?," or laughing with other group members as "Miss Sophie" forces the group members (and me) to sing along with yet another Kenny Rogers song. Folks who normally were feeling isolated in their struggles with voices and visions now have a place to come, feel safe, and most importantly be themselves. The principles discussed in the previous chapters seem to help my clients to do just that. Below is a quick review of the various principles and how they can promote good outcomes for clients who attend groups for voice hearers.

Emotional Safety

All the facilitators with whom I spoke mentioned the importance of cultivating emotional safety within the groups. This mechanism of change appeared to foster the development of both attachment and empowerment within group members. Several facilitators indicated emotional safety starts with the cultivation of physical safety and the feeling of "containment" within the room. When clients felt physically safe and contained, the facilitators observed their clients were more willing to share with others, which leads to increased social connection. Fostering an environment of validation, according to many facilitators, increased the client's feeling of emotional safety which led them to feel less marginalized, less isolated, and more willing to connect with others in the group. The same number of facilitators stated encouraging an environment of respect through the use of non-pathologizing language, treating clients "like human beings," and respecting the clients' emotional boundaries, which increases clients' ability to attach to others and their own level of self-respect.

There is limited research regarding how the group room environment impacts clients who attend AVH groups. Ozerengin and Cowen (1974) explored how physical environment of a clinical setting impacts clients who have "psychosis"-related experiences, but this study did not specifically address the group room environment. However, current literature on AVH groups does extensively explore how cultivating elements related to emotional safety such as validation, "containment," and respect in AVH groups can lead to increases in clients' overall functioning (Dillon & Hornstein, 2013; Hendry, 2011; Jones, Marino, & Hansen, 2015; Oakland & Berry, 2015). Additionally, the current literature (Dillon & Hornstein, 2013 and Jones, Marino, & Hansen, 2015) regarding AVH groups also supports the necessity of AVH group facilitators receiving training so they are well-equipped to effectively work with this client population. Dillon and Hornstein (2013) specifically stated facilitator training "safeguards the well-being" of clients so they are not inadvertently harmed by the facilitator.

As a facilitator, I have noticed the importance of setting up the group room in a safe manner and attending to the clients' comfort levels with everything from the placement of chairs, access to the door, the temperature in the room, to if the makings for coffee are available for clients. Although I don't fuss or dote over clients, I pay attention to any changes in the group room, as I know they will elicit some form of response (negative or positive) from clients. Recently, my regular group room was unavailable, so the clients and I went to a smaller room. Immediately, I could see the discomfort amongst several clients based on their facial expressions and took quick inventory of the room. Only a few clients had quick access to the door while others were blocked by a table. I took a risk and asked the group, "Hey, I notice some of you look uncomfortable. Is it because you don't have access to the door easily?" Several clients agreed, looked surprised I noticed, and asked to move closer to the door. As a group, we discussed why having access to a door might be important and why being blocked from doors could be triggering for some people. I follow these guidelines with setting up my group room for Hearing Voices Groups:

- Keep the chairs in a circle but allow folks to sit where they want (e.g., up against the wall).
- Make sure the door handle is easy to use (a small but very important factor for many folks who have been held against their will).
- Use a group room with windows and natural light—it makes the space feel more open.
- Have coffee, cups, filters, creamer, coffee pot, and coffee maker available. (Also, routinely clean the coffee pot.) My group clients *LOVE* coffee, and group does not begin until coffee is made. We also celebrate birthdays in my group with cupcakes (diabetes and low-fat diets be damned!).

Emotional safety or perceived lack thereof prevented me from sharing my voice hearing experiences with other clients in the hospital, therapists, family, and friends. When I attended the ISPS Conference in 2015 and saw how voice hearers were treated with respect, my shame about my lived experience began to slowly dissolve. As I discussed my lived experience with trusted mentors and a very calm and compassionate therapist (who no joke would be played by Maya Rudolph if my life were a movie), I cultivated a sense of internal emotional safety. Their non-anxious presence and thoughtful responses to my experiences modeled and informed the way I work with clients with voices and visions to this day. I know people are feeling safe in group when playfulness begins to emerge and group members spontaneously respond to one another. Recently, a client, James, who for the past six months has barely spoken a handful of words in group, has begun to share about his lived experiences, allowed his quirky sense of humor to show up in the room, and his range of facial expressions has expanded from blank and blanker to smiles, curiosity, and concern.

I knew James was truly opening up when he spontaneously introduced himself to a fellow group member (with a handshake!) and began teasing one of the other group members about her small stature. As we walked out of the group room, James sauntered next to her, looked down (she is a head shorter than he), and declared, "I feel like Lebron James next to you. I feel like Michael Jordan next to you. I feel so tall, like a basketball player!" The other client began laughing and smiling at him. (James is a sports lover, and when you get to know him he has a fantastic sense of humor. Hearing this exchange boosted my spirits because I knew he was coming out of his shell.) The next group, James discussed his fears of riding elevators and I volunteered to demonstrate the safety features on our building's elevator. After group, James trusted me to come onto the elevator, ride up one floor, and listen to me explain the emergency buttons. Miss Sophie, who is also afraid of elevators, chose to ride with us and promptly got her fingers knotted into her long hair. As I showed James the safety features of the elevator, Miss Sophie yelled out, "I'm stuck, I'm stuck, I'm stuck." Throughout this elevator safety lesson, James kept his composure, asked questions about the elevator buttons, and when we left the elevator, I helped Miss Sophie with untangling her fingers from her hair. Although this was a minor exchange, they were showing their trust in me to get them out of (various) troubling situations. Safety wasn't just in the group room, I was modeling safety in other areas of their lives. If folks can find a safe holding space with me, maybe they'll learn to recognize when safety shows up in the form of other trusted people in the community.

Flexibility

Most of the facilitators with whom I spoke indicated that flexibility is an important element for a successfully run group for this client population. Several group facilitators explained this mechanism of change can be promoted through:

- Arrangement of the chairs and allowing people to sit where they please
- Not being too authoritarian as a facilitator
- Not rigidly adhering to only one point of view regarding the etiology of psychosis-related experiences

The facilitators, who mentioned flexibility, believed incorporating this element into their groups leads to outcomes such as (1) increased sharing of ideas amongst group members, (2) allowing for different points of view, and (3) providing an emotionally corrective experience for group members. Dillon and Hornstein's (2013) observations on effective AVH groups support this data, for they indicated facilitators should take a "relaxed" approach, be "non-judgmental," and remain open-minded about group members' viewpoints regarding their experiences. These researchers stated: "because there is not judgment … for the first time in their lives [group members] can reveal what is happening inside them" (p. 290). Studies on clients' experiences in AVH groups also support the importance of being non-judgmental but did not specifically mention the term "flexibility" as a mechanism of change (Goodliffe, Hayward, Brown, Turton, & Dannahy, 2010; Newton, Larkin, Melhuish, & Wykes, 2007).

Being flexible as a group leader (for me) means finding a balance between setting basic group guidelines (e.g., adhering to a definitive start and end time to group sessions, reiterating the importance of respect between group members, and/or screening attendees prior to attending group) and creating a space in which clients can freely express themselves. Sometimes when I have new group members, particularly people who present with negative psychosis-related symptoms such as alogia, I bring along a hula hoop into the room and give folks the opportunity to hula hoop instead of doing a traditional check in. The "hooping" option is quite a hit with many clients and serves as a good icebreaker for the group members. However, I flex my authority if a client is demonstrating disrespectful behavior towards other group members. Several years back, a client began attending my group (and several of the other outpatient groups at the clinic where I work) and was evasive about experiencing voices and visions. (This occurred prior to my pre-screening days with this group.) He would inappropriately laugh while clients shared their experiences and make derogatory comments to clients during the group, and other group members, who knew him in the community, began to challenge his presence in the group. Finally, I point-blank asked this group member, "Do you *REALLY* have voices or visions? Do you have a loved one with these experiences?" He looked down and said, "No, I don't." (At this point, I had re-directed this particular gentleman several times over the past couple (read: two) groups, asking about his symptoms, inquiring after his seemingly inappropriate laughter, and reframing his harshly judgmental comments towards fellow group members.) I asked him, "What are you hoping to gain from attending this group?" The man replied, "I think I should leave." To which I said, "I think it best." Several group members approached after group and thanked me for "kicking him out."

I'm fairly non-judgmental but have little tolerance for people who foist their rigid and/or disrespectful opinions about voices/visions on fellow group members. Maybe this fellow had voices/visions but was too intimidated or self-loathing to share his experiences. Who knows … but I was not going to allow his brand of negativity in the group room. Voice hearers encounter enough jerks and judgment in their communities, so they shouldn't have to endure the same treatment in a group about voice hearing.

Group Process

Group process was also a central concept explored by many of the facilitators who participated in this study and appears to be another important mechanism of change for AVH groups. Several facilitators stated they focus on exploring and building relationships occurring within the room between clients. Several facilitators explained that focusing on group process encourages clients to form meaningful connections with others (both in and out of group). Facilitators can achieve this aim via role modeling authenticity—if you're just meeting a client or don't know him/her well, you shouldn't come at them in an overly warm manner. As coworkers and I like to joke, "You're coming in hot!" Too much warmth, gooey-eyed compassion, and tenderness can feel unbearable to many clients who come to these groups. To the client, you're some random therapist who doesn't know them or their troubles from a hole in the wall. I speak in a matter-of-fact tone, use everyday language to explain psychological terms/concepts, and remain mindful that my facial expression doesn't convey fear, pity, and/or condescension. Your authenticity as a facilitator will encourage clients to develop healthy and authentic connections to themselves and to other folks in the community. Approaches to avoid:

- Asking clients 1,001 questions at lightning speed.
- Don't be a voyeur. You don't need to know all the gory details, but instead, be curious!

- Avoid lecturing clients with a bunch of voice hearing-related facts and theories.
- Be mindful of the timing when asking triggering questions. There is such a thing as too much too soon.

Some facilitators also believed moving at a pace comfortable to the clients was important because the original experiences that led to psychosis-related experiences occurred because clients felt emotionally flooded. Working too quickly with clients, such as broaching painful topics too quickly or "poking around too much" (as my clients call it) can shut down the group, lead to client frustration, and/or decrease clients' willingness to connect with the facilitator or other group members. Remaining patient and meeting clients where they are encourages clients' willingness to share and prevents clients from feeling emotionally flooded. When listening to clients' stories for the first time, you'll need to balance between allowing someone "airtime" and not monopolizing the conversation. It can be challenging, and I have discovered many of my first-time attendees share a lot of their story with the group—such as type of hallucinations, past hospitalizations, etc. Many of these clients are sharing this part of themselves (e.g., voice hearing) with a group openly for the first time (outside of a family discussion, mental hygiene hearing, or a disruptive episode while hospitalized). Therefore, handle with care, don't rush the story, because (from lived experience) there is powerful healing in sharing one's story with a compassionate other(s).

The importance of group process with this client population is reflected in the literature as well. Facilitators who studied group members' experiences within AVH groups found that clients believe group process-related factors (e.g., their experiences being in relationships with others within the group, the support systems they build amongst group members) lead to good group outcomes such as feeling validated, connecting with others, and feeling supported (Dillon & Hornstein, 2013; Goodliffe, Hayward, Brown, Turton, & Dannahy, 2010; Hendry, 2011; Webb, 2011).

Self-Awareness

Promoting the development of increased self-awareness was identified by many facilitators as another mechanism of change. This process, according to several group leaders with whom I spoke, can be fostered by encouraging the clients to identify emotions connected to their "psychosis"-related experiences and/or by asking clients to reflect upon their own emotional process after a challenging group session. As I discussed in the self-awareness chapter, clients who have experienced trauma are at risk for their "mohawk of self-awareness" (Van der Kolk, 2014) to go offline (Arnsten, Raskind, Taylor, & Connor, 2015; Bluhm et al., 2009). Voice hearing, specifically hypervigilant and autobiographical subtypes, often develops in response to traumatic experiences (Dodgson & Gordon, 2009; Garwood, Dodgson, Bruce, & McCarthy-Jones, 2015). It then stands to reason that voice hearers are at risk for having under-developed self-awareness. Although anecdotal, I have found this to be true with my group members.

Encouraging clients to step towards exploring their voices in depth feels akin to asking my 7-year-old self to not cover her eyes during a scary movie. FORGET IT! TOO SCARY! However, encouraging clients to talk about the emotions related to their voices is a far easier sell for most group members. Many of my clients often like to remind me in group: "I don't hear voices anymore!" I understand this feeling—as I have made this distinction to friends, family, and colleagues so as to not appear weak. God forbid I identify with people who *STILL* hear voices. Nowadays, I have come to see voice hearing as on a spectrum—all of us hear voices. We have private internal conversations with ourselves to buy cereal at the grocery store, drop off dry cleaning, mentally chastise ourselves for eating too many donuts, or secretly criticize a loved one's choice in footwear/taste in music/excessive use of the word "literally." However, folks who come into my groups often have a harder time managing these internal conversations, and/or the content of the conversations may be ego-dystonic.

Nowadays, I explain to group clients about the spectrum of voice hearing and tell them "my voices" are now manageable. They fall into the "everyday" category of voices that most folks hear, but at one time they were unmanageable. This explanation normalizes clients' experiences and makes approaching their voices less frightening.

Clients can also learn from one another by observing other group members as they make meaning of *their* "psychosis"-related experiences and perhaps do so for themselves. Ultimately, many facilitators indicated promotion of self-awareness encourages clients to "decode" their psychosis-related experiences and figure out how their voices and visions fit within the narrative of their lives. These results are also supported by other studies (Webb, 2011; Newton, Larkin, Melhuish, & Wykes, 2007), which indicated that clients view learning to connect meaning to their voices and visions as a good group outcome and the CBTv approach to working with voices (Thomas et al., 2014; Lincoln & Peters, 2018).

Several of the facilitators with whom I spoke also stressed the importance of cultivating self-awareness *within themselves* so they do not inadvertently hinder or harm their group therapy clients. Dillon and Hornstein's (2013) observations on effective group facilitation for AVH groups supports this data as well, and they listed "self-awareness" as an important trait to possess for individuals who run AVH groups.

I can look back on the meaning behind all my voices and recognize the metaphors hidden within. Some voices reinforced the fears I had about the world based upon scary events in my life, other voices were fueled by anger towards certain abusers, and some voices were there to comfort me while I felt upset. Dissecting my voices took patience and a willingness to face my fears. The sharp mental sting of embarrassment and shame about my experiences as a voice hearer and the traumatic experiences which informed them have faded into just memories. No emotional charge occurs when I think about those times, talk about the experience with others, or write about it now. (But trust me—this journey took intention, effort, and work.)

Sticking with the process of unpacking the metaphors related to my voices (which were autobiographical) is something I am glad to have done. You don't have to be a voice hearer to run hearing voices groups, but (at the very least) get clear about your opinions regarding voice hearing and use supervision or consultation to discuss potential blind spots regarding psychosis-related symptoms. Do you have biases? Do you believe in recovery for folks with psychosis-related symptoms? What type of recovery can you imagine? Could a voice hearer become a good parent (child or pet), baker of amazing cupcakes, volunteer, friend, coworker, spouse, or (gasp) competent licensed clinical psychologist? I think so, but do you?

Empowerment

Over half the facilitators discussed the importance of cultivating empowerment within the group members and believe this factor to be a powerful mechanism of change because this client population is often treated in a dismissive fashion by others and/or frequently feel disempowered. Many facilitators indicated empowerment can be fostered by allowing clients to make decisions over various aspects of the group's structure (e.g., where to sit, developing group rules, being able to come/go from the room when feeling emotionally flooded). Clients were also encouraged by many facilitators to develop healthier relationships with their voices and/or to cultivate active coping skills, which individuals who run these groups believe can lead to group members feeling more in control over what is happening in their minds and having more agency within their lives. A couple of facilitators also stated a positive outcome related to empowerment is when clients were more assertive in their interactions with their treatment team (e.g., respectfully question or discuss treatment decisions with clinicians) and/or no longer viewed their treatment team "with blind adoration." The current literature on AVH groups supports these facilitators' beliefs on empowerment as well.

Several studies that explored what clients view as good group outcomes indicated they feel more empowered because of their participation in AVH groups as evidenced by clients' increased capacity to cope and develop improved relationships with their voices (Goodliffe, Hayward, Brown, Turton, & Dannahy, 2010; Hendry, 2011; Newton, Larkin, Melhuish, & Wykes, 2007).

Lived Experience

Finally, several facilitators stressed the importance of introducing recovery narratives of individuals who have lived experience into the group room. They indicated that this mechanism of change leads clients to feel an increased sense of pride amongst group members because they meet others (e.g., group members or the facilitator), see via videos, or learn through articles of people who have lived experience with "psychosis"-related experiences, are in recovery, and are living fulfilled lives. Facilitators also believed bringing in narratives of recovery instills hope in the group members as well. Additionally, many with whom I spoke encouraged facilitators to receive training through the Hearing Voices Network, which is run by voice hearers, because exposure to these individuals teaches new facilitators that recovery is possible. The literature on clients' views regarding mechanisms of change for AVH groups explores and supports the concept of encouraging "recovery"-minded thinking and introducing recovery narratives into the group room (Dillon & Hornstein, 2013; Hendry, 2011; Jones, Marino, & Hansen, 2015; Newton, Larkin, Melhuish, & Wykes, 2007; Webb, 2011).

Sharing my own lived experiences in this book, with friends, and with colleagues was at first nerve-racking. I started small with a few people beyond my immediate inner circle (family, therapist, friends) and told a few trusted colleagues. They already knew me professionally and/or as a doctoral student, so their opinion was not (I hoped) too biased by this new information. Eventually, I shared my story with colleagues (if relevant) and clients (again, if relevant to their personal growth). Talking about my own voice hearing and hospital stay, according to feedback from my clients in the voices group, is edifying. As one female client explained, "You get it! You know what it's like and aren't just getting your knowledge from textbooks." If you want to run a voices group, share the narratives of others with the group. There are plenty of wonderful stories of lived experience to be shared!

Clinical Considerations and Future Directions

As more studies on this particular topic continue to emerge, conducting a literature review comparing clients' and facilitators' ideas regarding mechanisms of change would be helpful to determine where the two groups' opinions intersect, where they do not, and possible reasons for why the opinions do not overlap. Additionally, all the facilitators with whom I spoke indicated that they sought out their own training outside of formal education (e.g., medical or graduate school) regarding how to conduct group therapy with this client population, and all facilitators recommended individuals who are interested in running AVH groups should seek out supervision and/or learn about this population through books, articles, conferences, workshops, or conferences. Classes and conferences recommended by facilitators are not readily available or easily accessible because they may require participants to travel out of state or to another country. Therefore, organizations that provide continuing education units for mental health providers in multiple cities should offer coursework on group facilitation for this client population to encourage more people to facilitate AVH groups. Presently, no major continuing education provider in the United States offers workshops on facilitation of AVH groups.

Conclusions

I initially became curious about this topic because several colleagues and I were hoping to start an AVH group at the community mental health agency where we worked. This book developed out of my personal interest in the topic of voice hearing, a clinical need to know how best to work effectively to facilitate an AVH group and to create the type of guide my fellow colleagues and I longed for when I was looking to start an AVH group several years ago. My hope is this study will encourage other researchers to conduct similar studies about facilitation of AVH groups and inspire people to facilitate AVH groups. This client population—and I include myself in this category—is often misunderstood, dehumanized, and stigmatized.

I recognize this view of clients, who struggle with psychosis-related experiences, is well entrenched in society, but perhaps making AVH groups more commonplace in mental health agencies, hospitals, and communities can (at the very least) begin to change the conversation amongst mental health professionals and society in general regarding how psychosis-related experiences are discussed, viewed, and treated in the years to come.

Summary Points

- Flexibility is important in groups. It helps with increased sharing of ideas and allows for expression of different views on the etiology of experiences. Also, flexibility can provide an environment conducive to corrective emotional experiences.
- Group process can help with building healthy attachments and allow for authenticity amongst others (including the facilitator), and can help minimize emotional flooding.
- Empowerment can be encouraged by developing active coping skills, encouraging healthier relationships with one's voices, and creating a sense of agency regarding treatment decisions.
- Self-awareness within groups can help make meaning of voices/visions. Clients can work toward becoming more emotionally self-aware, and a facilitator's increasing self-awareness can increase their sensitivity toward clients.
- Safety is important in the group setting. It can help develop increased attachment to others, minimize emotional flooding, promote self-respect, and decrease feelings of isolation.
- Discussing lived experiences can allow for a sense of hope for clients and facilitators, develop a sense of pride in oneself, normalize experiences, and promote a recovery narrative.

References

Arnsten, A., Raskind, M., Taylor, F., & Connor, D. (2015). The effects of stress exposure on prefrontal cortex: Translating basic research into successful treatments for post-traumatic stress disorder. *Neurobiology of Stress, 1*, 89–99.

Bluhm, R. L., Williamson, P. C., Osuch, E. A., Frewen, P. A., Stevens, T. K., Boksman, K., Neufeld, R. W., Theberge, J., & Lanius, R. A. (2009). Alterations in default network connectivity in posttraumatic stress disorder related to early-life trauma. *Journal of Psychiatry and Neuroscience, 34*(3), 187–194.

Dillon, J., & Hornstein, G. A. (2013). Hearing voices peer support groups: A powerful alternative for people in distress. *Psychosis, 5*(3), 286–295.

Dodgson, G., & Gordon, S. (2009). Avoiding false negatives: Are some auditory hallucinations an evolved design flaw? *Behavioral and Cognitive Psychotherapy, 37*(3), 325–334.

Garwood, L., Dodgson, G., Bruce, V., & McCarthy-Jones, S. (2015). A preliminary investigation into the existence of a hypervigilance subtype of auditory hallucination in people with psychosis. *Behavioral and Cognitive Psychotherapy, 43*(1), 52–62.

Goodliffe, L., Hayward, M., Brown, D., Turton, W., & Dannahy, L. (2010). Group person-based cognitive therapy for distressing voices: Views from the hearers. *Psychotherapy Research, 20*(4), 447–461.

Hendry, G. L. (2011). *What are the experiences of those attending a self-help hearing voices group: An interpretive phenomenological approach.* University of Leeds.

Jones, N., Marino, C., & Hansen, M. (2015). The hearing voices movement in United States: Findings from a national survey of group. *Psychosis, 8*(2), 106–117.

Lincoln, T. M., & Peters, E. (2018). A systematic review and discussion of symptom specific cognitive behavioural approaches to delusions and hallucinations. *Schizophrenia Research, 203*, 66–79.

Newton, E., Larkin, M., Melhuish, R., & Wykes, T. (2007). More than just a place to talk: Young people's experiences of group psychological therapy as an early intervention for auditory hallucinations. *Psychology & Psychotherapy: Theory, Research & Practice, 80*(1), 127–149.

Oakland, L., & Berry, K. (2015). "Lifting the veil": A qualitative analysis of experiences in Hearing Voices Network groups. *Psychosis, 7*(2), 119–129.

Ozerengin, M. F., & Cowen, M. A. (1974). Environmental noise level is a factor in the treatment of hospitalized schizophrenics. *Diseases of the Nervous System, 35*(5), 241–243.

Thomas, N., Hayward, M., Peters, E., van der Gaag, M., Bentall, R. P., Jenner, J., Strauss, C., Sommer, I. E., Johns, L. C., Varese, F., García-Montes, J. M., Waters, F., Dodgson, G., & … McCarthy-Jones, S. (2014).

Psychological therapies for auditory hallucinations (voices): Current status and key directions for future research. *Schizophrenia Bulletin, 40*(Suppl. 4), S202–212.

Van der Kolk, B. (2014). *The body keeps the score. Brain, mind, and body in the healing of trauma.* New York: Penguin Books.

Webb, J. (2011). *Hearing voices: Coping, resilience and recovery.* University of Leeds.

INDEX

For Product Safety Concerns and Information please contact our EU representative GPSR@taylorandfrancis.com
Taylor & Francis Verlag GmbH, Kaufingerstraße 24, 80331 München, Germany

www.ingramcontent.com/pod-product-compliance
Ingram Content Group UK Ltd.
Pitfield, Milton Keynes, MK11 3LW, UK
UKHW022202190926
475702UK00003B/152

* 9 7 8 1 1 3 8 5 0 0 6 3 1 *